Editorial Project Manager
Eric Migliaccio

Editor in Chief
Karen J. Goldfluss, M.S. Ed.

Cover Artist
Sarah Kim

Illustrator
Clint McKnight

Art Coordinator
Renée Mc Elwee

Imaging
James Edward Grace

Publisher
Mary D. Smith, M.S. Ed.

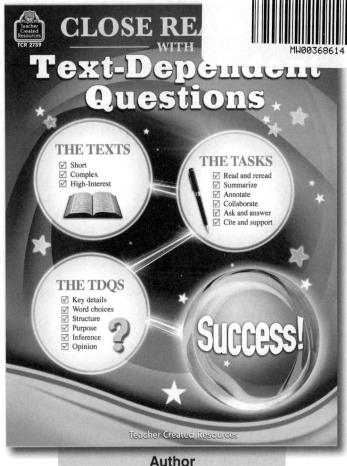

TCR 2739

CLOSE READING
WITH
Text-Dependent Questions

THE TEXTS
- ☑ Short
- ☑ Complex
- ☑ High-Interest

THE TASKS
- ☑ Read and reread
- ☑ Summarize
- ☑ Annotate
- ☑ Collaborate
- ☑ Ask and answer
- ☑ Cite and support

THE TDQS
- ☑ Key details
- ☑ Word choices
- ☑ Structure
- ☑ Purpose
- ☑ Inference
- ☑ Opinion

Success!

Teacher Created Resources

Author
Ruth Foster, M.Ed.

For the Lexile measures of the reading passages included in this book, visit *www.teachercreated.com* and click on the Lexile Measures button located on this resource's product page.

For correlations to the Common Core State Standards, see pages 95–96 of this book or visit *http://www.teachercreated.com/standards*.

Teacher Created Resources, Inc.
12621 Western Avenue
Garden Grove, CA 92841
www.teachercreated.com
ISBN: 978-1-4206-2739-8

© 2017 Teacher Created Resources, Inc.
Made in U.S.A.

Table of Contents

Section I Units

Each unit in this section includes a Close-Reading Passage, a page of Close-Reading Tasks, and two pages of Text-Dependent Questions.

Section II Units

Each unit in this section includes a Close-Reading Passage and a page of Peer-Led Tasks.

Overview

What Is Close Reading?

Close reading is thoughtful, critical analysis of a text. Close-reading instruction gives your students guided practice in approaching, understanding, and, ultimately, mastering complex texts. This type of instruction builds positive reading habits and allows students to successfully integrate their prior experiences and background knowledge with the unfamiliar text they are encountering.

There are certain factors that differentiate close-reading instruction from other types of reading instruction. These factors include the types of **texts** used for instruction, the **tasks** students are asked to perform, and the **questions** they are expected to answer. For detailed information on these factors, see "A Closer Look" on pages 4–5.

What Are Text-Dependent Questions?

Text-dependent questions (TDQs) can only be answered by referring explicitly back to the text. They are designed to deepen the reader's understanding of the text, and they require students to answer in such a way that higher-level thinking is demonstrated. To be most effective, TDQs should address all that a reading passage has to offer; the questions asked should prompt students to consider the meaning, purpose, structure, and craft contained within the text.

How Is This Guide Organized?

The units in *Close Reading with Text-Dependent Questions* are divided into two sections. Each of the twenty **Section I Units** (pages 8–87) is a four-page unit.

Page 1 **Close-Reading Passage**	This page contains a short, complex, high-interest reading passage. Parts of the passage are numbered for easy reference, and space for annotation is provided in the left margin and between lines of text.
Page 2 **Close-Reading Tasks**	Students are guided to read the passage, summarize it, reread and annotate it, and meet with a partner to discuss and define the author's word choices.
Page 3 **Text-Dependent Questions**	Students are asked to display a general understanding of the text, locate key details within it, cite evidence, and begin to use tools such as inference.
Page 4 **More TDQs**	Students examine the structure of the text and the author's purpose. They form opinions and use evidence to support and defend claims. A research prompt encourages choice, exploration, and cross-curricular connections. (**Note:** Monitor students' Internet research for content appropriateness.)

Each of the two **Section II Units** (pages 88–91) contains two pages.

Page 1 **Close-Reading Passage**	This page contains a short, complex, high-interest reading passage. Parts of the passage are numbered for easy reference, and space for annotation is provided in the left margin and between lines of text.
Page 2 **Peer-Led Tasks**	This page guides groups of students through a series of peer-led tasks in which each member is assigned a different role. Students become teachers to one another as they work together to analyze a text.

A Closer Look

Close Reading with Text-Dependent Questions focuses on the three main components of close-reading instruction: the **texts** students are asked to read, the **tasks** they are instructed to perform, and the **text-dependent questions (TDQs)** they are expected to answer thoughtfully and accurately.

The Texts

✓ short
✓ complex
✓ high-interest
✓ multi-genre

Not all texts are appropriate for close-reading instruction. Passages need to be written in a manner that invites analysis and at a level that requires slow, careful, deliberate reading. The texts in this guide achieve these goals in a number of ways.

- **Length:** Close-reading passages should be relatively short because the rigorous work required of students could make longer passages overwhelming.

Each unit in this guide contains a one-page passage of about 375–425 words. This is an ideal length to introduce and explore a subject, while allowing students of this age to conduct an in-depth examination of its content and purpose.

- **Complexity:** The best way to foster close reading of informational or fictional text is through text complexity. Writing achieves a high level of text complexity when it fulfills certain factors. The **purpose** of the text is implicit or hidden in some way, and the **structure** of the text is complex and/or unconventional. The **demands** of the text ask students to use life experiences, cultural awareness, and content knowledge to supplement their understanding. The **language** of the text incorporates domain-specific, figurative, ironic, ambiguous, or otherwise unfamiliar vocabulary.

The passages in this guide contain all of these different types of language and ask students to decipher their meanings in the context of the parts (words, phrases, sentences, etc.) around them. The passages meet the purpose and structure criteria by delaying key information, defying reader expectations, and/or including unexpected outcomes — elements that challenge students to follow the development of ideas along the course of the text. Students must combine their prior knowledge with the information given in order to form and support an opinion.

- **Interest:** Since close reading requires multiple readings, it is vital that the topics covered and style employed be interesting and varied. The passages in this resource will guide your students down such high-interest avenues as adventure, invention, discovery, and oddity. These texts are written with humor and wonder, and they strive to impart the thrill of learning.

- **Text Types and Genres:** It is important to give students experience with the close reading of a wide variety of texts. The passages in this guide are an equal mix of fiction and nonfiction; and they include examples and/or combinations of the following forms, text types, and genres: drama, poetry, descriptive, narrative, expository, and argumentative.

- **Lexile-Leveled:** A Lexile measure is a quantitative tool designed to represent the complexity of a text. The passages featured in this resource have been Lexile-leveled to ensure their appropriateness for this grade level. For more information, visit this resource's product page at *www.teachercreated.com*.

A Closer Look *(cont.)*

The Tasks

- ✓ read and reread
- ✓ summarize
- ✓ annotate
- ✓ collaborate
- ✓ connect
- ✓ illustrate
- ✓ cite and support
- ✓ ask and answer

An essential way in which close-reading instruction differs from other practices can be seen in the tasks students are asked to perform. This resource focuses on the following student tasks:

- **Read and Reread:** First and foremost, close reading requires multiple readings of the text. This fosters a deeper understanding as the knowledge gained with each successive reading builds upon the previous readings. To keep students engaged, the tasks associated with each reading should vary. When students are asked to reread a passage, they should be given a new purpose or a new group of questions that influences that reading.

- **Annotation:** During at least one reading of the passage, students should annotate, or make notes on, the text. Annotation focuses students' attention on the text and allows them to track their thought processes as they read. It also allows students to interact with the text by noting words, phrases, or ideas that confuse or interest them. When writing about or discussing a text, students can consult their annotations and retrieve valuable information.

> For more information about annotation, see pages 6–7 of this guide.

- **Additional Tasks:** Collaboration allows students to discuss and problem-solve with their partner peers. An emphasis is placed on demonstrating an understanding of unfamiliar words in context and applying academic vocabulary in new ways. Throughout, students are prompted to cite evidence to support claims and reinforce arguments. Often, students are asked to illustrate written information or connect text to visuals. A section of peer-led activities (pages 88–91) encourages students to ask and answer peer-generated questions.

The TDQs

- ✓ general
- ✓ key details
- ✓ word choice
- ✓ sequence
- ✓ structure
- ✓ purpose
- ✓ inference
- ✓ opinion

Text-dependent questions (TDQs) emphasize what the text has to offer as opposed to the students' personal experiences. This helps students focus on the text — from the literal (what it says) to the structural (how it works) to the inferential (what it means).

The TDQs in this resource ask students to demonstrate a wide range of understanding about the text. There is a progression from questions that ask for general understanding to those that require deeper levels of focus. The first question or two are relatively easy to answer, as this promotes student confidence and lessens the possibility for discouragement or disengagement. Subsequent questions delve into increasingly higher-order involvement in the text. Students are asked why a passage is written the way it is and if they feel that the author's choices were ultimately successful. This type of instruction and questioning not only makes students better readers, it also makes them better writers as they consider the decisions authors make and the effects those choices have on the text and the reader.

All About Annotation
Teacher Instructions

Annotation is the practice of making notes on a text during reading, and it is a crucial component of the close-reading process. It allows students to more deeply dissect a text and make note of the parts that intrigue or excite them, as well as the parts that confuse or disengage them. Annotation gives students a tool with which to interact with the text on their terms and in ways specific to their needs and interests.

Tips and Strategies

☑ This resource has been designed to give your students the space needed to annotate the reading passages. Extra space has been included in the margin to the left of the passage. In addition, room has also been added between each line of text, with even more space included between paragraphs.

☑ Share the student sample (page 7) to give your students an idea of what is expected of them and how annotation works. This sample only shows three basic ways of annotating: circling unfamiliar words, underlining main ideas, and writing key details. Begin with these to ensure that students understand the concept. Additional responsibilities and tasks can be added later.

☑ Much like the skill of summarization requires restraint, so does annotation. Give students a goal. For example, tell them they can only underline one main idea per paragraph and/ or their key notes for each paragraph can be no more than five words in length. If these expectations aren't given, students might make too many notes, circle too many words, and underline too much text. This would make the text more difficult to read and create the opposite effect of what is intended.

☑ If you see that a majority of your students are circling the same unfamiliar words and noting confusion in the same areas of the text, spend more time and focus on these parts.

☑ Instruct students to reference their annotations when answering more complex questions, such as those inquiring about the structural and inferential elements of the text.

☑ Annotations can be used as an assessment tool to determine how well students are analyzing a text or even how well they are following directions.

☑ If students need more room to annotate, consider allowing them to affix sticky notes onto their pages and add notes in this way.

☑ As students become more fluent at the skill of annotating, increase their responsibilities and/or add new tasks. Here are a few examples to consider:

- ◆ Add a question mark (?) for information they find confusing.
- ◆ Add an exclamation point (!) for information they find surprising.
- ◆ Draw arrows between ideas and/or elements to show connections.
- ◆ Keep track of characters' names and relationships.
- ◆ Add notes about such elements of authorial craft as tone, mood, or style.

All About Annotation (cont.)
Student Sample

Annotation = making notes on a text as you read it

3 Basic Ways to Annotate a Text

Note key details.

In the left margin, write a few words that give key details from the paragraph. Your notes in this space should be brief. They should be five words or fewer.

Circle difficult words.

If you aren't sure what a word means, circle it. Once you determine its meaning, write the word's definition in the left margin and circle it.

Underline main ideas.

Find the main idea of each paragraph and underline it. The main idea gives the most important information the author is trying to tell you in that paragraph.

Buried Alive

head in bucket practice

hidden, blocked

1 Before Keizo Funatsu was buried alive, he did something. Time and time again he would put a white plastic bucket on his head and walk around. Funatsu wasn't the only one who walked around with a plastic bucket on his head. Other scientists and explorers did the same, as they all wanted to practice getting around with obscured vision.

explore Antarctica dogsleds

deadly

2 Funatsu was a dog trainer and part of an expedition to Antarctica. The expedition's goal was to use dog sleds to explore Antarctica. The team was only 16 miles away from completing their 3,725-mile journey. It was then that a daily chore almost became fatal.

Buried Alive

 Before Keizo Funatsu was buried alive, he did something. Time and time again he would put a white plastic bucket on his head and walk around. Funatsu wasn't the only one who walked around with a plastic bucket on his head. Other scientists and explorers did the same, as they all wanted to practice getting around with obscured vision.

 Funatsu was a dog trainer and part of an expedition to Antarctica. The expedition's goal was to use dog sleds to explore Antarctica. The team was only 16 miles away from completing their 3,725-mile journey. It was then that a daily chore almost became fatal.

 He went to feed the dogs after the team had set up camp. Although this may sound like a simple task, it is a chore fraught with danger. Blizzards in Antarctica will strike fast and furiously, and when one did, it was impossible for Funatsu to see. Despite the close proximity to his teammates and the tents, Funatsu was helpless. Completely blinded and with the howling winds drowning out his voice, he was in danger. It was -25°F (-32°C), and his feet were beginning to freeze. If he didn't find shelter immediately, he would freeze to death.

 Furiously, Funatsu dug into the snow. He hollowed out a ditch and crawled inside. With blizzard winds in Antarctica often blowing at speeds near 200 miles per hour, it only took seconds for Funatsu to become covered in snow. He was buried alive, but he was out of the wind. Funatsu curled up in a ball to warm himself, but he didn't stay that way for long. Every 20 minutes or so, he would jump out and wave his hands hoping that someone would see him. The cold would always drive him back to his ditch.

 The other five team members were equally blinded by the snow. Still, they searched all night. To avoid getting lost themselves, they each held onto a section of a long rope. Marching and yelling, they could only hope that their efforts were not futile. It wasn't until morning that their efforts paid off. Funatsu thought he heard a voice. Although unsure, he made the decision to run toward the sound. He didn't know if he was running to his death or not until he spotted the shadowy figures of his teammates.

Your Name: _____   Partner: _____

Buried Alive (cont.)

First Silently read "Buried Alive." You might see words you do not know and read parts you do not understand. Keep reading! Determine what the story is mainly about.

Then Sum up only paragraphs 2–5 of the story. Write the main idea and most important information. If someone reads your summary, that person should know it is this story you are writing about, not a different story!

_____

_____

_____

_____

_____

_____

After That Read the story again. Use a pencil to circle or mark words you don't know. Note places that confuse you. Underline the main action or idea of each paragraph.

Next Meet with your partner. Help each other find these words in the text.

obscured   chore   fatal   proximity   futile

Read the sentences around the words. Think about how they fit in the whole story. Think about what the words mean, and then explain how the story helps you and your partner know the following facts. One answer is given for you.

a. When something is **obscured**, it is hidden or concealed. _____

_____

b. When something is in close **proximity**, it is near. _Even though Funatsu's_

teammates were in close proximity, they couldn't see or hear each other.

c. When someone does a **chore**, they are doing a task or job that needs to be done.

_____

_____

d. When something is **fatal**, it is deadly. _____

_____

e. When something is **futile**, it is useless. _____

_____

Your Name: _____

Buried Alive *(cont.)*

Now Answer the story questions below.

1. Why did Funatsu walk around with a white plastic bucket on his head?

_____

_____

Knowing what happened to Funatsu in the blizzard, do you think the white-bucket practice helped him? Why or why not?

_____

_____

_____

2. Do you think the blizzard described in the story was the first one Funatsu encountered? Use the clues given in the story to determine your answer. Explain which clues helped you decide.

_____

_____

_____

3. There are two idioms used in paragraph 3: "fraught with danger" and "strike fast and furiously." Choose one. Tell what it means in the way it is used in the story.

_____

_____

Which part or parts of the story help you know? _____

_____

4. Funatsu left his warm ditch every 20 minutes or so. What does this show about Funatsu's trust in his teammates?

_____

_____

Draw a picture to show what Funatsu's teammates might have looked like as they searched for him. In your picture, show how many teammates Funatsu had and how they avoided getting lost themselves.

Your Name: _____

Buried Alive *(cont.)*

Then   Reread the entire story one last time. Think about how paragraph 1 relates to the rest of the passage.

5. Write a very brief summary of paragraph 1.

_____

_____

_____

6. Why do you think the author began the story this way?

_____

_____

_____

7. Imagine if the author had begun the story with a paragraph of Funatsu's inner thoughts as he lay buried in the ditch for the first time. Write the first five lines of this new first paragraph.

_____

_____

_____

_____

_____

_____

Do you like the new introductory paragraph better? Why or why not? (You cannot be wrong, but you must explain.)

_____

_____

_____

_____

 Learn More   Use books or the Internet to find out five facts about Antarctica or Keizo Funatsu. On the back of this paper, write your information in paragraph form.

Case Solved

 While waiting for a client, Ava and Ethan were reading studiously. More often than not, the information Ava and Ethan gleaned from reading helped them solve cases. Currently, Ava was reading a novel set in modern day England, while Ethan was reading a history of cartography. The two budding detectives read raptly, eyes glued to the page, until they heard footsteps approaching their library desk.

 "I think my Aunt Birdie is being preyed on," said Suzanna, their first customer. "She's at my house right now showing my mom pictures this new friend of hers just brought back from her trip to London. Aunt Birdie's friend says she took all the photographs while on a tour. In every photograph, you can see the same bus driver holding the steering wheel with his right hand and pointing out the window with his left hand at Buckingham Palace, Big Ben, and all the famous tourist attractions. Aunt Birdie's friend says she can get my aunt on the same tour for just $500, but my aunt will have to pay in cash if she wants the budget price. My aunt can only afford the budget fare, but I just don't trust this friend."

 "You shouldn't," Ava said. "Here in the United States, we drive on the right side of the road. In England, they drive on the left. Our steering wheels are on the left-hand side of the car, while in England they are on the right. If a bus driver in England were to point out the window, he would use his right hand!"

 "My problem is with my Uncle Theo," said Rodney as Suzanna rushed off. "He wants to pay 1,000 dollars for a treasure map someone claims is 150 years old. My uncle says the treasure is worth at least a million dollars, so it's a good investment. Look at this photograph I took of the map and tell me what you think.

 As Ethan had just been reading about the science and making of maps, he was very interested. As he examined the map, Rodney said, "The letters are faded, but you can still read the country's name. The X marking the treasure is just under the *n* in *Iran*." It was at that instant that Ethan knew the map was a forgery. Persia wasn't renamed Iran until 1935.

Your Name: _____   Partner: _____

Case Solved *(cont.)*

First   Silently read "Case Solved." You might see words you do not know. It is likely there will be parts you do not understand. Keep reading! Determine what the story is mainly about.

Then   Sum up the story. Write the main idea and most important information. If someone reads your summary, that person should know it is this story you are writing about.

_____

_____

_____

_____

_____

_____

After That   Read the story again. Use a pencil to circle or mark words you don't know. Note places that confuse you. Underline the main action or idea of each paragraph.

Next   Meet with your partner. Help each other find these words in the text.

     client   studiously   gleaned   cartography   raptly

Read the sentences around the words. Think about how they fit in the whole story and what they mean. With your partner, explain how the story helps you and your partner know the following facts.

a. A **client** is a customer. _____

_____

b. When one is **studiously** doing something, one is not playing around. _____

_____

_____

c. When something is **gleaned**, it is gathered or picked up. _____

_____

d. **Cartography** is the science and making of maps. _____

_____

e. When one is **rapt**, one is fascinated and paying close attention. _____

_____

Your Name: _____

Case Solved *(cont.)*

Now   Answer the story questions below.

1. Why did Ethan know the treasure map was a forgery? _____

_____

_____

2. How do cars in England differ from those in the United States? _____

_____

_____

In the two boxes below, draw pictures to illustrate this difference. In the box labeled "England," draw a picture of where a driver would sit in a car in that country. Do the same for the box labeled "United States."

England	United States

3. In the first sentence of paragraph 2, Suzanna uses the expression "preyed on." What does she mean by this?

_____

_____

Which part or parts of the story help you know? _____

_____

4. What information are you given about the novel Ava was reading? _____

_____

Why might Ava **not** have been able to help Suzanna if novel had been set in 14th-century England?

_____

_____

_____

Your Name: _____

Case Solved *(cont.)*

Then   Reread the entire story one last time. Think about the author's purpose for writing the story as you read.

5. This story was written to entertain, but in the first paragraph, the author sends the reader a message about reading. What does the author want the reader to know?

_____

_____

How is that message reinforced in the rest of the story?

_____

_____

_____

_____

6. Do you think the author did a good job showing the importance of reading? Explain.

_____

_____

_____

Can you think of another example or time in your life when reading or having read something helped you know what to do?

_____

_____

_____

7. When crossing a street, children in the United States are taught to look **left**, **right**, **left** to make sure no cars are coming or turning into a crosswalk. Do you think this is what children in England are taught? Why or why not? Use evidence from the story in your answer.

_____

_____

_____

Learn More   Find out when the countries of Belize, Pakistan, and Bangladesh got their names. Then write a paragraph where someone finds out someone is lying or being tricked because of an incorrect name.

Bark Ranger

 The kid was trying to get to its mother, a wild mountain goat. The kid was distraught. It bleated frantically, but despite its desperate cries, it couldn't reach its mother. It couldn't because the nanny or doe goat was surrounded by 15 people all taking its picture. Park rangers who saw this disturbing incident wanted to prevent this kind of thing from happening again. To help them do their job, they called in a "Bark Ranger."

 Bark rangers are not people. They are canines. Gracie is a border collie currently being trained to be a bark ranger. Border collies are herding dogs. They are used by many sheep farmers to help herd their sheep. Gracie is not being trained to herd animals toward people. She is being trained to get behind the animals and drive them away from people.

 Park rangers explain that this is for the wild animals' own safety. For example, adult billy and nanny goats, as well as kids, were gathering in the highest parking lot cars could drive to in the park. The goats were congregating there because they were licking up the sweet-tasting antifreeze that had dripped from car engines and eating the trash that people had left behind. Antifreeze is poisonous, and no wild animal should become dependent on human waste.

 Park rangers had tried waving bags and firing empty shotgun shells into the air to keep the goats away from the parking lot. Nothing was as successful as Gracie, who was brought to the lot once or twice a week. As one of the park rangers explained, "To us she's a pretty little border collie, but to them she's a fuzzy little wolf-like thing."

 In one park, rangers were having problems with mother or doe deer that were overly aggressive in protecting their newborn fawns. Wildlife and people were just too close to each other. Bark rangers were called in to lend a hand — or in this case, a paw. The canines solved the problem in no time at all. Instead of 40 disturbing incidents each season, there were only four. Park rangers also liked that bark rangers helped them educate people. When people pet the dogs (who wear special vests), park rangers can remind the visitors why it is safer for all that wild animals keep their distance.

Your Name: _____ Partner: _____

Bark Ranger (cont.)

First Silently read "Bark Ranger." You might see words you do not know. It is likely there will be parts you do not understand. Keep reading! Determine what the story is mainly about.

Then Sum up the story. Write the main idea and most important information. If someone reads your summary, that person should know it is this story you are writing about.

_____

_____

_____

_____

After That Read the story again. Use a pencil to circle or mark words you don't know. Note places that confuse you. Underline the main action or idea of each paragraph.

Next Meet with your partner. Help each other find these words in the text.

distraught   bleated   frantically   canines   congregating

Read the sentences around the words. Think about how they fit in the whole story. Match the words to their synonyms. Tell which part of the story helped you know you are right.

a. A synonym for *dogs* is _____. I know because

_____

b. A synonym for *desperately* is _____. I know because

_____

_____

c. A synonym for *upset* is _____. I know because

_____

_____

d. A synonym for *meeting* is _____. I know because

_____

_____

e. A synonym for *cried* is _____. I know because

_____

_____

Your Name: _____

Bark Ranger (cont.)

Now   Answer the story questions below.

1. What is a mother mountain goat called? What is a baby mountain goat called?

mother mountain goat = _____

baby mountain goat = _____

2. Why were the goats congregating in the parking lot? _____

_____

_____

Why was this dangerous? _____

_____

_____

3. In the last paragraph, it says that the bark rangers were called in to "lend a hand — or in this case, a paw." What does the expression "lend a hand" mean in the way it is used here, and why does the author say that in this case one could say "lend a paw"?

_____

_____

_____

How does the story help you know? _____

_____

_____

_____

4. Are bark rangers helpful? Support your answer with evidence from the passage.

_____

_____

_____

_____

_____

Your Name: _____

Bark Ranger (cont.)

Then Reread the entire story one last time. As you read, think about how knowing what a bark ranger is helps you understand the passage.

5. In which paragraph do you find out what a bark ranger is? Check the box beside the correct paragraph number.

❑ 1 ❑ 2 ❑ 3 ❑ 4 ❑ 5

Is "bark ranger" an appropriate or good name? Explain.

_____

_____

_____

6. How often was Gracie brought to the parking lot to keep the goats away from people?

_____

Why do you think the park rangers were careful to only bring Gracie to the lot that many times? Why didn't they bring her there more often? (The answer is not in the story. You have to use clues from the story to guess why!)

_____

_____

_____

7. The passage is both informative (it gives you information) and persuasive (it makes the case and supports it with evidence). What tools does the author use to persuade you that bark rangers were a good solution to the problem? Name at least two different ways that the author tries to persuade the reader.

_____

_____

_____

_____

Learn More Look online or in books to find out more about border collies, other herding dogs, or Glacier National Park where Gracie worked. On the back of this paper, write a paragraph with at least five pieces of information about your chosen topic.

Updated Fairy Tale

 The week's reading assignment in Ms. McLean's reading class was an old fairy tale. It was called "The Emperor's New Clothes." It was written by a Dane named Hans Christian Anderson, but it had been translated into over 100 different languages. When Ms. McLean asked the students to summarize the story, the majority of the students raised their hands. Ms. McLean first called on Doug.

 "There was this emperor," Doug said, "who was proud as a peacock. All he cared about were his clothes. Two men came to the emperor and said they were tailors, and for a huge fee, they would weave some cloth and make the most stupendous suit in the world. The suit would cost a colossal sum of money, but it was worth the high price because the suit would be invisible to anyone who was stupid, incompetent, or unfit for their positions."

 Pleased with the recap so far, Ms. McLean gave permission to Joyce to continue. "The emperor was so vain that he immediately hired the men to make him a suit. The tailors pretended to weave some cloth and cut and sew a suit. There was nothing there, of course, but no one would admit it. The emperor would keep agreeing with the tailors that the suit was the finest thing he had ever seen. When the day came for the emperor to put on the suit, he still wouldn't admit that he couldn't see it, because he didn't want anyone to think he couldn't do his job or was stupid."

 Ms. McLean nodded to Michael to continue. "All of the king's advisors were afraid to say anything, either, because they didn't want anyone to think they were incompetent. People lined the streets to see the emperor in his new clothes. Everyone pretended to admire the suit until a little boy cried out, 'But he isn't wearing anything at all.'"

 Later that day, in the school's lunchroom, a student started teasing a new girl. "We're wearing identical white T-shirts. They're the same size and made of the same material, but mine is better. I know because I paid $300 for mine, and you only paid $10." All the students from Ms. McLean's class clustered around the new girl. They told her they were going to make her feel better. They were going to tell her a fairy tale called "The Emperor's New Clothes."

Your Name: _____   Partner: _____

Updated Fairy Tale *(cont.)*

First   Silently read "Updated Fairy Tale." You might see words you do not know and read parts
you do not understand. Keep reading! Determine what the story is mainly about.

Then   Sum up <u>paragraphs 1–4</u> only of the story. Write the main idea and most important
information. If someone reads your summary, that person should know it is this story you
are writing about.

_____

_____

_____

_____

_____

After That   Read the story again. Use a pencil to circle or mark words you don't know. Note places
that confuse you. Underline the main action or idea of each paragraph.

Next   Meet with your partner. Help each other find these words in the text.

  tailor   *fee*   stupendous   colossal   incompetent

Read the sentences around the words. Think about how they fit in the whole story. Think
about what the words must mean. Then mark each sentence as **T** (True) or **F** (False).
Explain which information in the story helped you and your partner know.

_____ **a.** A **tailor** fixes computers. _____

_____

_____ **b.** A **fee** is a payment. _____

_____

_____ **c.** When something is **stupendous**, it is awful. _____

_____

_____ **d.** Something **colossal** is huge. _____

_____

_____ **e.** An **incompetent** worker is really good at his job. _____

_____

Your Name: _____

Updated Fairy Tale *(cont.)*

Now   Answer the story questions below.

1. According to the tailors, who couldn't see the suit? _____

_____

_____

2. Why couldn't the king's advisors see the suit? _____

_____

_____

Do you think the king had good advisors? Tell why or why not. _____

_____

_____

_____

3. In paragraph 2, Doug says that the emperor is "proud as a peacock." What does this expression mean?

_____

_____

How does the story help you know? _____

_____

_____

4. Why might one argue that the two girls' T-shirts were the same? Use evidence from the story in your answer.

_____

_____

_____

Do you think one T-shirt is better than the other? Tell why or why not.

_____

_____

_____

Your Name: _____

Updated Fairy Tale *(cont.)*

Then   Reread the entire story one last time. As you read, think about how the last paragraph relates to the story.

5. Sum up the last paragraph.

_____

_____

_____

_____

6. How does this paragraph help to update the fairytale "The Emperor's New Clothes"?

_____

_____

_____

7. For the students in Ms. McLean's class, how do you think they were affected by reading a tale like "The Emperor's New Clothes"? Do you think the girl with the expensive T-shirt had ever read this tale? Use evidence from the story to support your claims.

_____

_____

_____

Write about a time when you knew something was wrong or not true but you didn't say anything because you worried that everyone else thought differently. If you can't think of a time or just want to make one up, feel free to do so. You can set your description in the past or in the present time.

_____

_____

_____

_____

 Learn More   Read the translated text of "The Emperor's New Clothes" in a book or on the Internet. On the back of this paper, write a paragraph in which you tell which story you like better, the original or the updated one.

Eaten!

 A famous author and illustrator once received a card with a small drawing on it from one of his young fans. The author found the card charming. The author often answered children's fan letters quite hastily, but the author was so charmed by this particular card that he took his time with his response. Lingering over it, he drew a picture of a Wild Thing before writing on it, "Dear Jim: I loved your card." Soon after, the author received a letter from Jim's mother. In the letter, Jim's mother said, "Jim loved your card so much, he ate it." Who was this famous author, and how did he respond?

 The author was Maurice Sendak. Sendak is probably most well-known for his book *Where the Wild Things Are*. In this childhood favorite, a little boy named Max threatens to eat his mother up after she calls him "Wild Thing." Max is sent to bed without eating anything, and thus he begins an imaginary adventure into the land of where the wild things are.

 Sendak wasn't upset that the drawing he had lingered over and taken his time with had been eaten. Sendak was pleased! As he later recounted, "That to me was one of the highest compliments I've ever received. He didn't care that it was an original Maurice Sendak drawing or anything. He saw it, he loved it, he ate it." Despite Sendak's response, one can't help but wonder how the grown Jim feels today. After all, if the drawing still existed, it might be worth a king's ransom!

 Sendak's reaction to his artwork being consumed is a clue to what kind of person he is, but so too is his book *Pierre*. Although lesser known, this rhyme is a rollicking tale of a boy who keeps saying he doesn't care. At one point, even when *"A hungry lion paid a call | He looked Pierre right in the eye | And asked him if he'd like to die,* | Pierre responds over and over with *I don't care!* Consequently, the lion eats Pierre.

 Sendak, being so kind-hearted and compassionate, could never end a tale on such a gruesome note. In the story, Pierre's parents are alerted to their son's location, and they find the lion sick in bed, muttering that he doesn't care. They rush the lion to a doctor, Pierre is saved, and the lion stays on as a guest. Just like Sendak, the now wiser Pierre cares.

Your Name: _____ Partner: _____

Eaten! *(cont.)*

(First) Silently read "Eaten!" You might see words you do not know. It is likely there will be parts you do not understand. Keep reading! Determine what the story is mainly about.

(Then) Sum up the story. Write the main idea and most important information. If someone reads your summary, that person should know it is this story you are writing about.

_____

_____

_____

_____

(After That) Read the story again. Use a pencil to circle or mark words you don't know. Note places that confuse you. Underline the main action or idea of each paragraph.

(Next) Meet with your partner. Help each other find these words in the text.

hastily   lingered   recounted   compassionate   rollicking

Read the sentences around the words. Think about how they fit in the whole story. Define the words. Which information from the text helped you figure out their meanings?

Word	Definition	Information That Helps
hastily		
lingered		
recounted		
compassionate		
rollicking		

Your Name: _____

Eaten! *(cont.)*

(Now)   Answer the story questions below.

1. Why are Pierre's parents so sure the lion ate him?

_____

_____

2. Do you think Sendak expected Jim to eat the drawing of the Wild Thing? Defend your answer with evidence from the story.

_____

_____

_____

3. At the end of paragraph 3, you are told that the drawing might be worth "a king's ransom." What is meant by this expression?

_____

Which part of the story helped you know?

_____

_____

4. Does the story about Pierre end on a gruesome note? Tell why or why not. Quote words from the story as part of your answer.

_____

_____

_____

Draw two frames of a cartoon to illustrate two scenes from *Pierre*. Use the information in the story to guide you.

Your Name: _____

Eaten! *(cont.)*

Then Reread the entire story one last time. Think about important details versus minor details.

5. There is one paragraph that starts off with an important detail but is then filled with details that are not as important to the rest of the story. They could have not been written, and the story still would have made sense. Which paragraph is it? Check the correct box.

❏ 1 ❏ 2 ❏ 3 ❏ 4 ❏ 5

Do you think the author included all the minor details in hopes that it would help you realize who Sendak is? Explain.

_____

_____

_____

6. How does the title of the story relate to the events contained within it?

_____

_____

_____

What if the title of the story were titled "Max"? Why isn't "Max" a good title for the story?

_____

_____

7. Imagine if the title of the story were "Maurice Sendak." Do you think the author would have changed the way she wrote the first paragraph if this were the title? Tell why or why not.

_____

_____

_____

Learn More Find five autobiographical facts about Maurice Sendak by looking online or in books. Write them out in numbered form. Or, find the words to *Pierre* (in a book or online) and tell why you think it is or isn't a good story.

_____

_____

_____

Why Day

 "They lack collarbones and their spines are more flexible. Blood vessels known as capillaries are located near the thin skin. He was a patriot. The moisture doesn't evaporate as quickly."

 The students in Ms. Trivia's class looked at her with mouths agape. They sat stunned, wondering if their teacher had gone crazy. They weren't able to shut their mouths and compose themselves until Ms. Trivia explained. "I decided today is going to be 'Why Day.' I just answered four 'Why?' questions. The first question is, 'Why do cats always land on their feet?' Because cats don't have collarbones, they can easily bend and rotate their bodies more than other animals. That fact coupled with the knowledge that their spine is more flexible than other animals explains it all."

 Ms. Trivia flexed her fingers before straightening them. Then she said, "Now it's back to the grind and time for you to put your thinking caps on. You have to match the 'Why?' questions to the answers I gave you previously." The students didn't have time to even groan before Ms. Trivia rattled off the questions. "Why do racehorses run counterclockwise? Why are lips red? Why don't sweaty hands smell as bad as sweaty feet?"

 Eloise called out excitedly, "Lips are red because blood vessels known as capillaries are located near the thin skin of your lips!" Ms. Trivia was so pleased with Eloise's correct match that she decided not to reprimand Eloise for forgetting to raise her hand. She didn't scold Hadrian, either, when he forgot to raise his hand. She was so pleased that he, too, matched a question correctly to its answer. He knew that both hands and feet have more than 250,000 sweat glands. He also knew that bacteria feed off the water and salt of sweat, and it is the waste product of bacteria that stinks. Sweat evaporates on hands before bacteria can feed, whereas feet are often wrapped in socks and shoes, making it harder for the moisture to evaporate.

 Kanye, an American history buff, knew that a patriot named William Whitley opened the first circular race track in America in 1780. To rebel against the British and show his love for his country, Whitley had his horses run in the opposite direction than British race horses. His ran counterclockwise. The tradition remained even when runners and cars took to the track.

Your Name: _____   Partner: _____

Why Day *(cont.)*

First Silently read "Why Day." You might see words you do not know. It is likely there will be parts you do not understand. Keep reading! Determine what the story is mainly about.

Then Sum up the story. Write the main idea and most important information. If someone reads your summary, that person should know it is this story you are writing about.

_____

_____

_____

_____

_____

_____

_____

After That Read the story again. Use a pencil to circle or mark words you don't know. Note places that confuse you. Underline the main action or idea of each paragraph.

Next Meet with your partner. Help each other find these words in the text.

lack   flexible   patriot   agape   reprimand

Read the sentences around the words. Think about how they fit in the story. Think about what the words must mean and decide how the story helps you know the following things:

a. When you **lack** something, you don't have much of it. _____

_____

_____

b. Something that is **flexible** can bend easily. _____

_____

c. A **patriot** loves his or her country. _____

_____

d. When your mouth is **agape**, it is opened widely. _____

_____

e. When one is **reprimanded**, one is scolded. _____

_____

Your Name: _____

Why Day *(cont.)*

Now   Answer the story questions below.

1. If a cat falls from atop a piece of furniture, how will it most likely land?

_____

Why? Use information from the story to answer.

_____

_____

_____

_____

2. In races held in Britain, in which direction do the horses run around a track? Prove your answer with evidence from the story.

_____

_____

_____

3. In paragraph 3, Ms. Trivia says, "Now it's back to the grind and time for you to put your thinking caps on." What does she mean when she uses the expressions "back to the grind" and "put your thinking caps on"?

_____

_____

Which parts of the story helped you know?

_____

_____

_____

4. If feet and hands have the same number of sweat glands, why do sweaty feet smell worse than sweaty hands? Explain the entire process that leads to feet being smellier than hands.

_____

_____

_____

_____

Your Name: _____

Why Day (cont.)

Then) Reread the entire story one last time. Think about how paragraph 1 relates to the rest of the passage.

5. When do you find out why you were given the information in paragraph 1? Check the box.

   ❑ 1   ❑ 2   ❑ 3   ❑ 4   ❑ 5

   In that paragraph, what does Ms. Trivia say so that you understand the information?

   _____

   _____

   _____

6. If you had only read paragraph 1 and you had a choice, would you have continued reading the story? Tell why or why not. You cannot be wrong because it is your opinion, but you must explain your answer.

   _____

   _____

   _____

7. Every answer to the "Why?" questions is true. Is the story fact or fiction? Explain.

   _____

   _____

   _____

   What do you think was the author's purpose for writing the story this way?

   _____

   _____

   _____

**Learn
More**) Look up the meaning of the word *trivia*. Then find an interesting bit of trivia and write out a "Why?" question and answer that Ms. Trivia might use on her next "Why Day".

   _____

   _____

   _____

Sampling Snot

 Karina Acevedo-Whitehouse tied herself to a boat. Then she leaned overboard as far as she could. She was trying to catch something. Despite the danger she put herself into, it wasn't working. Karina was not accomplishing her goal. Karina was a veterinarian and a conservation biologist. She was trying to collect whale snot.

 Scientists knew very little about the fungi, bacteria, and viruses that lived inside whales. This was due to the marine mammal's massive size. It's not so easy to take a blood sample or any other kind of specimen from an animal swimming free in the ocean. It's especially difficult when it's from an animal so huge and powerful that one turn of its body or flip of its tale could mean a scientist's untimely death.

 When a whale spouts, warm snot, vapor, and other biological materials come rocketing out of its blowhole. After seeing some huge whale 'blows' in the Gulf of California, Karina realized that if she could obtain a snot specimen, she could use it to see what was living inside a whale's lungs. When Karina's initial attempts failed, she didn't give up. Instead of leaning over the boat, she attached petri dishes to long poles that she could hold over blows. This worked fine for whales like the grey and sperm whales, because they didn't mind being close to a boat. For shyer whales, such as the blue whale, Karina used toy helicopters that were remote-controlled.

 Karina's idea and sampling techniques proved to be a step in the right direction. Other scientists began looking at whale snot, too. They used it to analyze the mammal's DNA and microbiome. They used it to check the whale's stress and pregnancy hormones.

 Today, poles and toy helicopters are old hat. A special drone called a SnotBot is being tried. The SnotBot can fly closely along the water. When a whale surfaces and blows, the drone automatically moves into position and collects its bounty. It then returns to the research boat to drop off its treasured samples before immediately going back out. The drone can find its way back to the research boat even when it is half a mile away. This means that scientists no longer have to chase in their noisy boats after whales. The SnotBot can do all the collecting while the whales are left in peace.

Your Name: _____   Partner: _____

Sampling Snot *(cont.)*

First   Silently read "Sampling Snot." You might see words you do not know. It is likely there will be parts you do not understand. Keep reading! Determine what the story is mainly about.

Then   Sum up the story. Write the main idea and most important information. If someone reads your summary, that person should know it is this story you are writing about.

_____

_____

_____

_____

_____

_____

After That   Read the story again. Use a pencil to circle or mark words you don't know. Note places that confuse you. Underline the main action or idea of each paragraph.

Next   Meet with your partner. Help each other find these words in the text.

massive   specimen   obtain   initial   bounty

Read the sentences around the words. Think about how they fit in the whole story. Discuss how the author helped you know what the words meant. Then pick one word each. Make sure you each choose a different word. Fill in the blanks.

a. My partner's word: _____

My partner thinks that in this passage, the word must mean _____

_____

I agree because in the passage, _____

_____

_____

b. My word: _____

I think that in this passage, this word must mean _____

_____

My partner agrees because in the passage, _____

_____

Your Name: _____

Sampling Snot (cont.)

Now   Answer the story questions below.

1. What are scientists using whale snot for? Give specific examples from the text.

_____

_____

_____

_____

2. What advantages does the SnotBot have over a pole or a toy helicopter?

_____

_____

_____

3. In paragraph 5, it says that poles and toy helicopters are "old hat." What does this expression mean in the way it is used here?

_____

_____

How does the story help you know? _____

_____

_____

4. Are all whale types equally comfortable around people? Defend your answer using evidence from the text.

_____

_____

_____

Your Name: _____

Sampling Snot *(cont.)*

Then Reread the entire story one last time. As you read, think about how information about Karina is spread throughout the story.

5. Analyze the seven sentences in paragraph 1. Why do you think the author wrote each part of paragraph 1 in the way she did? What is the author's purpose for the following:

   a. the first sentence by itself? _____

   _____

   b. the first five sentences together? _____

   _____

   c. the sixth sentence? _____

   _____

   d. the seventh (last) sentence? _____

   _____

6. In which other paragraphs is Karina mentioned? Check each box that applies.

   ❑ 2   ❑ 3   ❑ 4   ❑ 5

   Did weaving in the story of an actual scientist help you understand how science works? Explain.

   _____

   _____

   _____

7. Why is paragraph 2 important? What purpose does this paragraph serve in the story?

   _____

   _____

   Why is paragraph 5 important? What purpose does this paragraph serve in the story?

   _____

   _____

Learn More Draw a picture of what you think the SnotBot drone might look like. Then compare your picture to what can be seen on the Internet.

Fair Swap?

 Janelle (*jovially*): I can't believe what a great bargain I just got! I swapped my new tennis shoes for this magic lamp!

Kyle (*aghast*): I'm shocked! How could you be so foolish as to trade your tennis shoes for that piece of junk? There's definitely no such thing as a magic lamp.

 Janelle (*defensively*): The peddler seemed so honest, and he promised me that I would get three wishes."

Duane (*curiously*): What would you wish for?

Janelle (*ruefully*): Now that Kyle has made me regret what I did, I wish I had new tennis shoes again.

 Kyle (*inquisitively*): You said you got three wishes. I'm curious about what else you would wish for.

Janelle (*longingly*): I would wish for a huge diamond, and I wish I could talk to Abraham Lincoln. I love jewelry, and I would interview President Lincoln because I have to write a report on him. Instead of looking up all the information I need, I could just ask him for it directly."

Young-su (*scolding as he rushes in*): Janelle! I found your new shoes at the park. I raced over here to return them. How could you be so careless!

Kyle (*laughingly*): And now it's time for the diamond!

 Young-Su (*curiously*): That reminds me, when and how did you turn your front yard into a baseball field? It looks like a perfect diamond. The sod, bases, and pitcher's mound look amazing."

Janelle (*fearfully*): I don't like the way my wishes are turning out. I wish I had never wished for anything!

 Duane (*consolingly*): I'm sure everything that has happened is just a strange coincidence. Your wishing has nothing to do with what has occurred."

Kyle (*nervously looking out window*): Maybe so, but I'll be on pins and needles until we find out who the tall man with the beard and top hat is at the door."

Your Name: _____   Partner: _____

Fair Swap? *(cont.)*

First Silently read "Fair Swap?" You might see words you do not know. It is likely there will be parts you do not understand. Keep reading! Determine what the play is mainly about.

Then Sum up the play. Write the main characters, actions, and most important information. If another person reads your summary, they should know it is this play you are writing about.

_____

_____

_____

_____

_____

_____

_____

After That Read the play again. Use a pencil to circle or mark words you don't know. Note places that confuse you. Look at all the words in the parentheses that describe the character's tone of voice when they are speaking. Use what the characters say to help you define the words.

Work with a partner to write short phrases or sentences you might say if you were speaking with the same tones of voice.

a. jovial

b. aghast

c. defensively

d. ruefully

e. inquisitively

f. longingly

g. scolding

h. consolingly

i. nervously

Your Name: _____

Fair Swap? *(cont.)*

Now   Answer the questions below.

1. What were Janelle's three wishes? What did she want? Draw a picture of each.

Wish #1	Wish #2	Wish #3
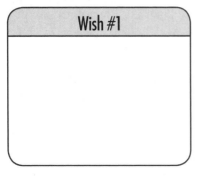		

2. What is Janelle's front yard like, and how do you find out this information?

   _____

   _____

   _____

   Do you think Janelle knew beforehand? Defend your answer with information from the text.

   _____

   _____

   _____

3. At one point, Kyle uses the expression "on pins and needles." What does he mean?

   _____

   _____

   How does the story help you know that you are right?

   _____

   _____

4. Do you think Janelle likes to do research in the library or on her computer? Defend your answer with evidence from the text.

   _____

   _____

   _____

Your Name: _____

Fair Swap? (cont.)

Then Reread the entire play one last time. Think about how the cast of characters and information about the setting is missing.

5. When a playwright writes a play, the introduction is a list of characters with a brief notation about who they are and a description of the setting and time. In the box below, write out these introductory parts.

> ### Cast of Characters (in order of appearance)
>
> _____ _____
>
> _____ _____
>
> ### Setting and Time
>
> _____
>
> _____

6. Read the play out loud. Make your voices match the tone in parentheses. Then read the play out loud again, but this time without varying your voices. Which reading was better? Tell why.

_____

_____

7. Is the lamp magical? Is it really Abe Lincoln at the door? Or is there a practical explanation? It is up to you! Write a continuing dialog for the play. Each character must speak at least once. (Your dialogue does not have to finish the play. It just has to continue it.)

_____

_____

_____

_____

_____

_____

 Learn More Research someone's history by thinking of five questions and then interviewing them. Present your information by writing the answers under the questions or in an oral report.

King of Sting

 It was described as "pure intense, brilliant pain. Like walking over flaming charcoal with a three-inch nail embedded in your heel." On a scale from 1 to 4, it was ranked a 4. The description and ranking were given by Dr. Justin Schmidt. Schmidt is an entomologist. There are hundreds of thousands of insect species, but Schmidt focuses on the order *Hymenoptera*. This order includes bees, ants, and wasps.

 Schmidt wanted to develop a scale that could be used when describing the pain of insect stings. In order to develop the scale, Schmidt allowed himself to be stung 2,500 times by various stinging insects. The scale, called the Schmidt Sting Pain Index, describes sting pain and ranks it on a scale from 1 to 4. The insect that merited the above description was a bullet ant.

 Bullet ants live in an area from southern Brazil up to Nicaragua. The ants usually nest on the bottom of the forest floor, but they make their ways up to the top of the tree canopy where they forage for prey. Black and stocky, the ants may look like sluggards, but they are the opposite. They are fast and acrobatic, and they should be avoided.

 In one interview, Schmidt said, "I don't consider myself all that tough. Crazy? Well, that's in the eye of the beholder. You probably can make an argument that I am crazy, but I enjoy what I do." In another interview, Schmidt said his favorite stinger is "the harvester ant." These ants have the most toxic known insect venom. If bitten, the pain is extremely long lasting. One will start sweating, and the hair on one's arm will stand up like the hair on the back of a frightened dog's neck. As it is 40 times more potent than the venom of a Western Diamondback Rattlesnake, it is a good thing that the ant only has a tiny bit of venom.

 The average person may fear the harvester ant because of its sting, but Schmidt's focus is broader. He sees the mystery in the complex biochemistry. Although people have been studying the venom for over 35 years, scientists still can't account for all the neurological things that are unique to it.

Your Name: _____   Partner: _____

King of Sting (cont.)

First   Silently read "King of Sting." You might see words you do not know. It is likely there will be parts you do not understand. Keep reading! Determine what the story is mainly about.

Then   Sum up the story. Write the main idea and most important information. If someone reads your summary, that person should know it is this story you are writing about.

_____

_____

_____

_____

_____

After That   Read the story again. Use a pencil to circle or mark words you don't know. Note places that confuse you. Underline the main action or idea of each paragraph.

Next   Meet with your partner. Help each other find these words in the text.

embedded   entomologist   forage   sluggards   potent

Read the sentences around the words. Think about how they fit in the whole story. Discuss how the author helped you know what the words meant. Then pick one word each. Make sure you each choose a different word. Fill in the blanks.

a. My partner's word: _____

My partner thinks that in this passage the word must mean _____

_____

I agree because in the passage, _____

_____

_____

b. My word: _____

I think that in this passage this word must mean _____

_____

My partner agrees because in the passage, _____

_____

_____

Your Name: _____

King of Sting *(cont.)*

Now   Answer the story questions below.

1. Explain the process Schmidt used to develop his scale? _____

    _____

    _____

    Explain how the scale works. How many numbers does it have? What do the numbers mean?

    _____

    _____

2. Do entomologists study sharks? Check the correct box.   ❏ Yes   ❏ No

    Which information from the story helps you know your answer is correct?

    _____

    _____

    Do all entomologists study beetles? Check the correct box.   ❏ Yes   ❏ No

    Which information from the story helps you know your answer is correct?

    _____

    _____

3. In the first part of paragraph 4, Schmidt uses the expression "in the eye of the beholder." What does he mean?

    _____

    _____

    How does the story help you know? _____

    _____

    _____

4. What might happen to you if you are stung by harvester ants? Quote the part of the story that provides the answer.

    _____

    _____

    _____

Your Name: _____

King of Sting (cont.)

Then Reread the entire story one last time. Think about how the last paragraph relates to the rest of the story.

5. The last paragraph may not be as "thrilling" to read, but it gives a hint as to why it may be important that entomologists study stinging insects. Why is it important to study stinging insects? Use information from the story as part of your answer.

_____

_____

_____

6. The author compares the venom of one insect to the venom of a snake. How do they compare? In your answer, name the specific animals involved.

_____

_____

Do you think this comparison helped you understand how powerful the harvester ant venom is? Tell why or why not.

_____

_____

_____

7. In the interview information given in the story, Schmidt talks about whether or not he is tough or crazy. Choose a different word that you feel describes Schmidt and/or what he does for a living. Use information from the text to support and defend your choice.

I think Schmidt is _____, and here's why: _____

_____

_____

If you were given the chance to interview Schmidt, what one question would you ask him?

_____

_____

Learn More Research one of the insects mentioned in the story or any other in the order *Hymenoptera*. On the back of this paper, write a paragraph with at least five facts.

Good Luck Bat

 Samantha felt sick inside when she stepped up to bat. She knew it was going to be a disaster before the first pitch was even thrown. She was going to strike out as usual. Everyone knew it. The other team had smug sneers on their faces while Samantha's own team looked sad and dejected. Samantha swung listlessly and struck out.

 Samantha's uncle strode purposefully over to Samantha as she was hurriedly trying to brush away her tears. "You've got the wrong bat," he said, handing her a new one. "This one is special. I had it made from some wood from a tree that a sorcerer said had special powers." Samantha didn't believe in wizards or sorcery, but she knew her uncle was a scientist and explorer. He had made several trips deep into the Amazon jungle in search of medicinal plants. Perhaps one of the tribes with which he had come into contact knew something about the tree that other people didn't.

 No one expected Samantha to hit the ball the next time she was called to bat, but she swung energetically instead of listlessly. As the ball sailed out past the farthest outfielder, there was a moment of silence as everyone stared in astonishment. Then the screaming and yelling began, and it never stopped. Time after time, game after game, Samantha hit the ball hard each time she was at bat.

 After the second-to-last game of the season, as Samantha was carefully stowing her bat in her duffle bag, she was delighted to see her uncle. "I'm off to central Africa this time," he said, "but I wanted to watch you one more time before I left. You knocked my socks off! I'm simply amazed at what a great hitter you've become." When Samantha told her uncle that it was all due to his lucky bat, he got a peculiar expression on his face. "You're old enough to know there's nothing special about that bat," he said quietly. "You just lacked confidence, and I wanted you to believe in yourself. Samantha, I purchased that bat at the store right here in town."

 When it was time for the ultimate game of the season, Samantha thought about what her uncle had said to her. Striding up to the plate, she stood ready for the first pitch. When she swung, she swung hard and mightily, but all she hit was air.

Your Name: _____   Partner: _____

Good Luck Bat (cont.)

First Silently read "Good Luck Bat." You might see words you do not know. It is likely there will be parts you do not understand. Keep reading! Determine what the story is mainly about.

Then Sum up the story. Write the main idea and most important information. If someone reads your summary, that person should know it is this story you are writing about.

_____

_____

_____

_____

_____

_____

After That Read the story again. Use a pencil to circle or mark words you don't know. Note places that confuse you. Underline the main action or idea of each paragraph.

Next Meet with your partner. Help each other find these words in the text.

dejected   listlessly   stowing   purchased   ultimate

Read the sentences around the words. Think about how they fit in the whole story. Define the words. Which information from the text helped you and your partner figure out the meaning of the words?

Word	Definition	Information That Helps
dejected		
listlessly		
stowing		
purchased		
ultimate		

Your Name: _____

Good Luck Bat *(cont.)*

Now   Answer the story questions below.

1. How does Samantha's hitting ability change through the course of the story?

    _____

    _____

    _____

2. Why did Samantha believe the bat might have special powers? Include at least two pieces of information from the story in your answer.

    _____

    _____

    _____

    _____

3. Samantha's uncle tells her that she knocked his socks off.

    a. What does the expression "knock your socks off" mean? _____

        _____

        How does the story help you know? _____

        _____

        _____

    b. "You knocked my socks off" is an idiom. An idiom is an expression that has come to have a different meaning than its literal meaning. How do you know that when Samantha's uncle says, "You knocked my socks off!" he is using an idiom?

        _____

        _____

        _____

4. Use evidence from the story to prove that the bat was not lucky.

    _____

    _____

    _____

    _____

Your Name: _____

Good Luck Bat (cont.)

Then   Reread the entire story one last time. As you read, think about what you find out about the bat as the story progresses.

5. In which paragraph do we find out where Samantha's uncle bought the bat? Check one.

❑ 1   ❑ 2   ❑ 3   ❑ 4   ❑ 5

Why do you think Samantha's uncle waited to tell her the truth?

_____

_____

6. Now that you have read the entire story, think about the genre into which it fits.

   a. Choose one genre that best describes the story. (If you are not familiar with these genres, look closely at the first word in each one for a clue.)

❑ science fiction   ❑ realistic fiction   ❑ magical realism

Explain your answer. _____

_____

_____

   b. If you had answered this question before you read paragraph 5, would your answer be different? Explain.

_____

_____

_____

7. As you read the story, did you begin to accept the idea that the bat had magical powers? If so, how did the author achieve this? If not, why not? Also, tell how you felt at the end. Were all of your questions answered?

_____

_____

_____

Learn More   Look in books or online to find out more about baseball bats. On the back of this paper, write a paragraph about what you find out. Your paragraph should have at least five pieces of information.

Blubber How-To

 Blubber is simply amazing. Blubber is why a whale, walrus, or a polar bear can swim through ice-cold water and stay warm. Blubber is a thick layer of fat that acts as insulation. It is what prevents an animal's body heat from escaping into the cold, frigid water. In some animals, like dolphins or polar bears, the layer of blubber may only be a few inches thick. In other animals, like some whales, the thickness of the blubber layer may measure a foot.

 Blubber has a dual purpose and does more than act as insulation. It is also a source of stored energy. Food may be scarce, especially during dark winter months. Scientists have found that some whales go months without eating. When food is hard to find, these whales survive by living off the blubber they saved up in the previous months. There are times half of an animal's body weight may be blubber!

 To comprehend how well blubber can protect one from the cold, you can conduct a simple experiment. First, you need to get some vegetable shortening, which is a type of fat. You will also need two zipper-lock sandwich bags, a spoon, and a bowl of ice water with ice cubes. Once you have all your materials, you can perform the experiment.

 The first step is to use the spoon to fill one bag one-third full of shortening. Then take the second bag and turn it inside out. That may seem crazy, but there is method to this madness. Next, slip the inside-out bag into the bag filled with shortening. Spread the shortening all around so it is trapped between the two bags like a layer of blubber.

 Once you have made your blubber mitt, slip your hand into the inside-out bag and zip up both bags around your hand as tightly as possible. Next, put both of your hands into the bowl of ice water. (One hand should be bare, and the other should be wearing the blubber mitt.) You will quickly notice that one hand stays much warmer than the other. Before removing your hand from the blubber mitt, you might think for a moment about the huge difference just a thin layer of fat makes. Imagine if you were insulated by a foot of blubber all around! You might be so warm that you might want to add more ice cubes to the water!

Your Name: _____   Partner: _____

Blubber How-To (cont.)

First | Silently read "Blubber How-To." You might see words you do not know. It is likely there will be parts you do not understand. Keep reading! Determine what the story is mainly about.

Then | Sum up the story. Write the main idea and most important information. If someone reads your summary, that person should know it is this story you are writing about.

_____

_____

_____

_____

_____

After That | Read the story again. Use a pencil to circle or mark words you don't know. Note places that confuse you. Underline the main action or idea of each paragraph.

Next | Meet with your partner. Help each other find these words in the text.

insulation   frigid   dual   scarce   conduct

Read the sentences around the words. Discuss how they fit in the story and how the author helped you know their meaning. Then pick one word each. Fill in the blanks.

a. My partner's word: _____

My partner thinks that in this passage the word must mean _____

_____

I agree because in the passage, _____

_____

_____

b. My word: _____

I think that in this passage this word must mean _____

_____

My partner agrees because in the passage, _____

_____

_____

Your Name: _____

Blubber How-To (cont.)

Now   Answer the story questions below.

1. Why can one say that blubber is "dual purpose"? _____

_____

_____

_____

2. Which hand stays warmer in the experiment? _____

_____

Why? _____

_____

_____

_____

3. In paragraph 4, it says that there is "method to this madness." What is meant by this expression the way it is used here?

_____

_____

How does the story help you know? _____

_____

_____

4. How full are you told to fill the bag with shortening? Shade in the figure to the right to show.

Considering what you do with the bag, why do you think you aren't told to fill the bag two-thirds full or eight-ninths full?

_____

_____

_____

_____

_____

Full
8/9
7/9
6/9
5/9
4/9
3/9
2/9
1/9
Empty

Your Name: _____

Blubber How-To (cont.)

Then   Reread the entire story one last time.

5. A "how-to" is a type of story that tells you how to do something. This story is a very confusing how-to. Why?

_____

_____

Which paragraphs actually gave "how-to" information? Check the box beside all that apply.

❑ 1   ❑ 2   ❑ 3   ❑ 4   ❑ 5

6. Write a better "how-to." Use only the necessary information. Tell the steps needed.

Title: _____

Materials: _____

Steps: _____

_____

_____

_____

_____

If your "how-to" could contain one drawing, which step would you choose to illustrate? Why?

_____

_____

7. Think about the paragraphs that had nothing to do with the "how-to." Did they help to make you interested in doing the "how-to"? Tell why or why not.

_____

_____

_____

Learn More   Using the books or the Internet, find out five facts about an animal that needs blubber to help it survive. On the back of this paper, write out your information in paragraph form.

Banner in the Sky

 I looked at the book with the torn cover and yellowed pages in disgust. I had to spend the week at my grandfather's house, and I felt I was back in the Dark Ages. My grandfather didn't have a television set, a computer, a tablet, or even a smartphone! When I asked him what I could watch before I went to sleep, he handed me a book. I was so aggravated and irritated at the situation I found myself in that I wanted to blow my top.

 I was still angry, but out of sheer boredom I opened the book. It was called *Banner in the Sky*, and it was written in 1954 by James Ramsey Ullman. I didn't know how a book that old could be of any interest to me, but then I started to read.

 Sixteen-year old Rudi Matt has fled his tedious and boring job and is walking high in the Swiss Alps when he hears a desperate cry for help. A man has fallen deep into an icy crevasse, and he has been there for hours. At first, the man is relieved when he hears Rudi's voice, but then he realizes that Rudi is alone and doesn't have a rope. It will take hours for Rudi to get back to his village and get help, and by that time, the man will have frozen to death.

 The man accepts his fate, but Rudi takes off all of his clothes, ties them to his walking stick, and dangles the clothes "rope" over the rim of the crevasse. Rudi then lies down flat in the snow and braces himself for what is to come. As Rudi bears the weight of the man, his muscles scream out in agony. Rudi is sure his arms will be pulled out of his sockets. When the man finally climbs over the lip of the crevasse, he is astonished. He says, "But you're just a boy!"

 The man is a world famous mountain climber who had come to try to climb the highest peak in the Alps for the first time. The climber wants to tell everyone how Rudi saved his life, but Rudi explains that he climbs in secret because his mother doesn't want him to be a climber. Rudi had just explained to the flabbergasted climber that he was just a dishwasher when my grandfather asked me if it was time to turn out the light. I said, "Not until I find out if Rudi climbs the highest mountain!"

Your Name: _____ Partner: _____

Banner in the Sky (cont.)

First — Silently read "Banner in the Sky." You might see words you do not know. It is likely there will be parts you do not understand. Keep reading! Determine what the story is mainly about.

Then — Sum up the story. Write the main idea and most important information. If someone reads your summary, that person should know it is this story you are writing about.

_____

_____

_____

_____

_____

_____

After That — Read the story again. Use a pencil to circle or mark words you don't know. Note places that confuse you. Underline the main action or idea of each paragraph.

Next — Meet with your partner. Help each other find these words in the text.

   aggravated   tedious   crevasse   agony   flabbergasted

Read the sentences around the words. Think about how they fit in the whole story. Then match the words to their synonyms. Tell which part of the story helped you and your partner know you are right.

a. A synonym for *ravine* is _____. I know because

_____

b. A synonym for *dull* is _____. I know because

_____

c. A synonym for *astonished* is _____. I know because

_____

d. A synonym for *pain* is _____. I know because

_____

e. A synonym for *bothered* is _____. I know because

_____

Your Name: _____

Banner in the Sky (cont.)

Now Answer the story questions below.

1. Why doesn't Rudi go back to his village and get help? _____
   _____
   _____

2. How do the narrator's feelings about the book change? Defend your answer with evidence from the story.
   _____
   _____
   _____
   _____

3. In the first paragraph, the narrator says, "I wanted to blow my top." What is meant by this expression the way it is used here?
   _____
   _____

   Which part of the story helped you know?
   _____
   _____

4. Why was the famous mountain climber astonished that Rudi was just a boy? Give the details that show why the climber was astonished.
   _____
   _____
   _____
   _____

   Do you think his level of astonishment was more, less, or the same when he found out that Rudi didn't want him to talk about what happened? Your answer cannot be wrong, but you must explain.
   _____
   _____
   _____

Your Name: _____

Banner in the Sky *(cont.)*

Then Reread the entire story one last time. As you read, think about how the first two paragraphs relate to the rest of the passage.

5. After reading only the first two paragraphs, what do you know about the book the grandfather gave to the narrator?

_____

_____

If you had only read paragraphs 3 and 4, would you have known you were reading a recap of a book? Explain why or why not.

_____

_____

_____

6. Why didn't the boy think the book would interest him at first?

_____

_____

Think of a book that you thought would be of no interest to you, but you changed your mind after reading it. Tell why you thought it would be of no interest and what changed your mind.

_____

_____

_____

7. Why do you think the author of this story chose to tell a story within a story? What purpose do you think the author was going for? How successful do you feel the author was in accomplishing this purpose?

_____

_____

_____

 Learn More *Banner in the Sky* is fiction, but Ullman has said that many parts resemble the true story of the first ascent of the Matterhorn. Find out five facts about the Matterhorn or of any climbers who attempted it. On the back of this paper, write an informative paragraph on the subject.

Driverless Cars

 Back in the 1880s, "safety bicycles" replaced "high wheelers." Safety bicycles had two wheels of the same size, while high wheelers had one huge front wheel and one tiny back one. Since they were much easier to ride and less prone to mechanical problems, bicycles became very popular. People who were afraid of change objected to the safety bicycle. They claimed that they were morally hazardous. They said they were dangerous because they would lead children into making bad decisions and cause them to spend less time reading. Before, children had to stay close to home. Now, in just 15 minutes, they could be miles away.

 I am going to defend driverless cars. Why then did I mention people's objections to safer bicycles? I did it to show that we should not fear innovation. Change is good! Despite the millions of bicycles being ridden by children, the world has not fallen apart. Children are still responsible and are still good decision-makers. They continue to read, and even if they can travel farther afield, they do turn around and ride back home.

 Henry Ford was the first to start producing cars on an assembly line. This method made cars more quickly and cheaply. One bank president said, "The horse is here to stay, but the automobile is only a novelty—a fad." As the car is well over 100 years old, it is no longer a novelty. It may not be new, but new inventions are making it better and safer.

 Cars today are safer than ever before. They are built to withstand crashes, and they are equipped with seatbelts and airbags. Despite all these safety features, there are still accidents. Statistics show that the majority of accidents are due to driver error.

 There is a proverb that reads "necessity is the mother of invention." We need to eliminate or at least reduce driver error, and that can be done with driverless cars. There are fearful naysayers who cry danger and harm to society at the thought of this new technology, but we must not listen to them. We must remember that we have sent men to the moon and spacecraft to Mars. We have the will and the power to computerize our cars in such ways that they can drive themselves. We must not be afraid of change. We must embrace it.

Your Name: _____   Partner: _____

Driverless Cars (cont.)

First Silently read "Driverless Cars." You might see words you do not know. It is likely there will be parts you do not understand. Keep reading! Determine what the story is mainly about.

Then Sum up only paragraphs 2–5 of the story. Write the main idea and most important information. If someone reads your summary, that person should know it is this story you are writing about.

_____

_____

_____

_____

_____

After That Read the story again. Use a pencil to circle or mark words you don't know. Note places that confuse you. Underline the main action or idea of each paragraph.

Next Meet with your partner. Help each other find these words in the text.

   prone   hazardous   innovation   novelty   eliminate

Read the sentences around the words. Think about how they fit in the whole story. Define the words. Which information from the text helped you figure out the meaning of the words?

Word	Definition	Information That Helps
prone		
hazardous		
innovation		
novelty		
eliminate		

Your Name: _____

Driverless Cars (cont.)

Now Answer the story questions below.

1. What is the difference between a "high wheeler" bicycle and a "safety bicycle"? In the boxes, draw a picture of each. On the lines below, use your own words to describe the differences.

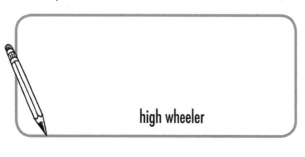

_____

_____

_____

2. What is the author's argument in favor of driverless cars?

_____

_____

_____

3. In the last paragraph, the writer quotes the proverb that states "necessity is the mother of invention." What is meant by this proverb?

_____

_____

Which part of the story helped you know? _____

_____

4. What does the author think is holding us back when it comes to driverless cars?

_____

_____

How do you know? _____

_____

Your Name: _____

Driverless Cars *(cont.)*

Then Reread the entire story one last time. Think about how paragraph 1 relates to the rest of the passage.

5. What is paragraph 1 mainly about? _____

_____

_____

What is its purpose? _____

_____

_____

6. After the introduction, the writer asks a rhetorical question. A rhetorical question is a question that is asked to make a point. The person who asks the question does not expect you to answer it. The person will answer it himself/herself. If the person doesn't answer it, that is because the answer is obvious. Which rhetorical question did the writer ask?

_____

_____

Was the answer to the rhetorical question a fact or an opinion? How do you know?

_____

_____

7. Taxi services are beginning to use driverless cars. Write out this rhetorical question: "Will I get in a driverless car when it pulls up to the curb?" Then answer it and tell why.

_____

_____

_____

_____

_____

Learn More Find out how people feel about driverless cars. Ask five people in each of the following age ranges: ages 3–19, ages 20–39, and ages 40 and up. Write a few lines in which you tell why you think you got the results you did.

First Contact

 "Am I going to get an arrow in my neck?" Dr. Paulo Bueno worried. Despite his trepidation, he didn't show his fear. He didn't allow himself to think about how the arrows of the men standing before him had been dipped in poison that oozed from the skin of poison dart frogs.

 Dr. Bueno was an anthropologist. Anthropology is the study of past and present humans, and Dr. Bueno's specialty was studying isolated tribes. Dr. Bueno had set up camp near the border of a reserve the government had set aside for isolated tribes. The reserve was a huge tract of land that was very remote and far away from any cities, towns, or roads. People who lived in the reserve were so isolated that they had never had contact with outsiders. They had no idea that there was a modern world out there. They had never seen a paved road, a car, an electric light, or even a shoe.

 Dr. Bueno had meant to walk just a little ways from camp, but when he tried to retrace his steps, he couldn't. Completely disoriented, he had no idea where he was or what direction to go in. All he saw was a wall of dark green. Then suddenly, without any hint that they had been there before, people emerged from the dense forest and surrounded him.

 Feeling his life was hanging by a thread, Dr. Bueno did what the men surrounding him wanted. When they motioned with their spears for him to move, he tripped and stumbled, but he moved. By the time they came to a small clearing with a few scattered huts made of branches and leaves, Dr. Bueno was drenched in sweat, scratched and bleeding, and covered in insect bites. Looking around, Dr. Bueno saw children playing with pet monkeys and a woman gnawing on the tail of a caiman. Another woman was cutting up an anteater with a stone knife.

 Sheena looked at the man that had come to the village. Strange skins covered his body, and the most peculiar objects were in front of his eyes. Instead of toes, his feet were solid clubs. When Sheena asked her father what they were going to do with him, Sheena's father said, "We will have to take care of him. A jaguar was about to pounce on him, and he just stood there. He is nothing more than a baby with a very weak mind."

Your Name: _____   Partner: _____

First Contact (cont.)

First — Silently read "First Contact." You might see words you do not know. It is likely there will be parts you do not understand. Keep reading! Determine what the story is mainly about.

Then — Sum up only paragraphs 1–4 of the story. Write the main idea and most important information. If someone reads your summary, that person should know it is this story you are writing about.

_____

_____

_____

_____

_____

_____

After That — Read the story again. Use a pencil to circle or mark words you don't know. Note places that confuse you. Underline the main action or idea of each paragraph.

Next — Meet with your partner. Help each other find these words in the text.

trepidation   anthropologist   isolated   remote   disoriented

Read the sentences around the words. Think about how they fit in the whole story. Think about what the words must mean. Then mark each sentence as **T** (True) or **F** (False). Tell which information in the story helped you and your partner know.

_____ **a.** When one feels **trepidation**, one is afraid. _____

_____

_____ **b.** An **anthropologist** studies caimans. _____

_____

_____ **c.** When one is **isolated**, one is apart from others. _____

_____

_____ **d.** When something is **remote**, it is close and easy to get to. _____

_____

_____ **e.** When one is **disoriented**, one knows where one is. _____

_____

Your Name: _____

First Contact *(cont.)*

Now Answer the story questions below.

1. Most likely, what were "the strange skins," "peculiar objects in front of eyes," and "solid clubs" referred to in paragraph 5? Draw a picture of each. Write the word by which you would call each object.

"strange skins"	"objects in front of eyes"	"solid clubs for feet"
Your word	**Your word**	**Your word**
_____	_____	_____

2. In what physical state was Dr. Bueno in when he arrived in the village? Quote parts of the story in your answer.

   _____

   _____

   Did his condition help to make a good impression on Sheena and the others who saw him for the first time? Explain.

   _____

   _____

3. In paragraph 4, it says that Dr. Bueno felt that his life was "hanging by a thread." What does the expression "hanging by a thread" mean?

   _____

   How does the story help you know?

   _____

   _____

4. Do you think the woman cutting up the anteater had ever seen a bicycle? Defend your answer using evidence from the story.

   _____

   _____

Your Name: _____

First Contact *(cont.)*

Then   Reread the entire story one last time. As you read, think about how the last paragraph relates to the story.

5. Sum up the last paragraph.

_____

_____

_____

_____

6. This story is realistic fiction. Explain why, using details from the story in your explanation.

_____

_____

_____

_____

Why do you think the author chose to write the story this way?

_____

_____

_____

_____

7. How do you think your opinion of the anthropologist might differ from Sheena's?

_____

_____

Who is correct, you or Sheena? Explain your answer.

_____

_____

Learn More   Find out more about isolated tribes by looking in books or online. Decide if the government should spend money on keeping loggers and oil companies from their refuges.   On the back of this paper, write a paragraph explaining what you think and why.

Leg Burn

 She had started at the lowest point in North America. The location was Badwater Basin in Death Valley, California. The elevation was 282 ft. (86 m) below sea level. Her ultimate goal was Mount Whitney, the highest point in the contiguous 48 United States. The distance was 135 miles, and she only had 48 hours to complete it if she didn't want to be disqualified from the race. Amy Palmiero-Winters wasn't disqualified, but she stopped short.

 Amy had to drop out just shy of 100 miles, because she was suffering from third-degree burns on one of her limbs. Third-degree burns are severe burns that cause damage through every layer of the skin. Without surgery, these wounds heal with severe scarring and contracture. Amy had to stop if she was to save what remained of her leg.

 Amy was running with a prosthetic leg. Amy had been injured while riding her motorcycle; and after 30 surgeries, her leg needed to be amputated. Amy's prosthetic was a blade, and the heat from the road rose through her artificial leg and caused the burns. In the Badwater Ultramarathon — or "the world's toughest foot race," as it has been billed — runners must brave blazing air temperatures as high of 130°F. The black road surface is even hotter. For Amy, the extreme heat was burning her alive.

 Although Amy had to drop out, she didn't give up. Once adjustments were made to her prosthesis, she entered the grueling race again. When Amy crossed the finish line in the allotted time, she became the first female amputee to ever finish this challenging run.

 Amy ran her first race when she was only eight years old. The shoes she wore were borrowed, and she had stuffed them with toilet paper to make them fit better. She crossed the finish line, but she was dead last. When Amy reflects back on how she lost, she says, "I didn't feel bad because I came in last. It sparked something inside of me."

 That spark kept Amy running to keep up with her two older brothers. It kept her running track and cross country in high school. It kept her running while making deliveries for her family's drive-in restaurant. It kept her running even after her leg was amputated.

Your Name: _____   Partner: _____

Leg Burn *(cont.)*

First Silently read "Leg Burn." You might see words you do not know. It is likely there will be parts you do not understand. Keep reading! Determine what the story is mainly about.

Then Sum up the story. Write the main idea and most important information. If someone reads your summary, that person should know it is this story you are writing about.

_____

_____

_____

_____

_____

After That Read the story again. Use a pencil to circle or mark words you don't know. Note places that confuse you. Underline the main action or idea of each paragraph.

Next Meet with your partner. Help each other find these words in the text.

      disqualified   prosthetic   billed   grueling   allotted

Read the sentences around the words. Think about how they fit in the whole story. Discuss how the author helped you know what the words mean. Then pick one word each. Make sure you each choose a different word. Fill in the blanks.

a. My partner's word: _____

My partner thinks that in this passage the word must mean _____

_____

I agree because in the passage, _____

_____

_____

b. My word: _____

I think that in this passage this word must mean _____

_____

My partner agrees because in the passage, _____

_____

_____

Your Name: _____

Leg Burn *(cont.)*

Now   Answer the story questions below.

1. Why would someone be disqualified from the Badwater race?

_____

_____

When Amy dropped out, do you think she had been running longer than five hours? Tell why or why not.

_____

_____

_____

2. If you burned yourself and got a blister, do you think that would be a second-degree burn or a third-degree burn? Defend your opinion with information from the text.

_____

_____

_____

_____

3. In the first sentence of the second paragraph, the expression "just shy of" is used. What does this expression mean here?

_____

How does the story help you know?

_____

_____

_____

4. Do you think Amy ran races in the time before the accident that led to the amputation of her leg? Support your answer with information from the story.

_____

_____

_____

_____

Your Name: _____

Leg Burn (cont.)

Then Reread the entire story one last time. As you read, think about how the story is divided into two parts.

5. Which paragraphs focus on the Badwater Ultramarathon? Check each box that applies.

   ❑ 1 ❑ 2 ❑ 3 ❑ 4 ❑ 5 ❑ 6

   Which paragraphs focus on Amy's start and interest in running? Check each box that applies.

   ❑ 1 ❑ 2 ❑ 3 ❑ 4 ❑ 5 ❑ 6

   Why do you think the author presented the information in this way?

   _____

   _____

6. The story is going to be rewritten so that the new first line will be "Amy was being burned alive." Using information from the story, write the next three lines of the new first paragraph.

   Amy was being burned alive. _____

   _____

   _____

   _____

   Do you think this new paragraph is a better way to start the story? Tell why or why not.

   _____

   _____

7. When Amy came in last, she said she didn't mind because it sparked something in her. What did Amy mean by this?

   _____

   _____

   Think of something you like to do. When and how did you become interested?

   _____

   _____

Learn More Look in books or online to find five pieces of information about the Badwater Ultramarathon, Amy Palmiero-Winters, or a blade prosthesis. On the back of this paper, write a paragraph about what you find out.

Three Months at 6°

 "I'm thinking of a very difficult and arduous job," Mr. Dang said to his class of sixth graders. "For three straight months, you have to stay in bed." The class burst out laughing when they heard this, but Mr. Dang put up a hand to quiet them. "Staying in bed may sound like a breeze, but when I say stay in bed, I'm not saying it figuratively. I'm saying it literally. You literally can't get out of bed for three straight months. It's a lot harder than it sounds, and to make it even more arduous, the bed is sloped downward at a six-degree angle."

 The students sat pensively for a few moments, and then they began to hammer Mr. Dang with questions. Mr. Dang was pleased with their queries, as all the questions showed that the students had listened to and then thought about what he said. Once again, he put up a hand to quiet them before telling them he would answer what questions he could.

 "First of all," he said, "The job was for NASA. As you all know, NASA is an acronym for the National Aeronautics and Space Administration. Scientists at NASA are investigating the long-term effects on the human body of living without gravity. One of their experiments had people lie at an angle of 6° for three months.

 "The people were paid about $18,000, but trust me: the participants earned it. They had to stay at a medical center, so they had people taking care of them, but they couldn't sit up or leave the bed. This means they were eating, trying to stay clean, and going to the bathroom all while lying down. They could watch television or work on their computers, but only while they were lying flat. Some of the participants got to exercise on a vertical treadmill, but not all of them. The vertical treadmill allowed people to run while suspended horizontally."

 The students were still talking about what Mr. Dang had told them at lunchtime. One of them had an idea, and soon the word was passed and everyone was in on it. After lunch, the students took their books and supplies and lay down on the floor of the classroom. When Mr. Dang asked them what was going on, all the students laughed and said, "For the rest of the day, we're going to practice being astronauts."

Your Name: _____   Partner: _____

Three Months at 6° *(cont.)*

First Silently read "Three Months at 6°." You might see words you do not know and read parts you do not understand. Keep reading! Determine what the story is mainly about.

Then Sum up <u>paragraphs 1–4 only</u>. Write the main idea and most important information. If someone reads your summary, that person should know it is this story you are writing about.

_____

_____

_____

_____

_____

After That Read the story again. Use a pencil to circle or mark words you don't know. Note places that confuse you. Underline the main action or idea of each paragraph.

Next Meet with your partner. Help each other find these words in the text.

arduous   literally   pensively   queries   acronym

Read the sentences around the words. Think about how they fit in the whole story. Then match the words to their synonyms. Tell which part of the story helps you and your partner know you are right.

a. A synonym for *thoughtfully* is _____. I know because

_____

_____

b. A synonym for *difficult* is _____. I know because

_____

_____

c. A synonym for *questions* is _____. I know because

_____

_____

d. A synonym for *factually* is _____. I know because

_____

_____

Your Name: _____

Three Months at 6° *(cont.)*

Now Answer the story questions below.

1. Why is NASA paying people to stay in bed? _____

_____

_____

What must one do to fulfill the conditions of the job?

_____

_____

_____

2. How did the students react when they first heard about the job?

_____

Do you think they reacted the same way after Mr. Dang gave them more information? Tell why you think so.

_____

_____

3. In paragraph 1, Mr. Dang says that it may "sound like a breeze." In paragraph 2, the students "hammer Mr. Dang." Choose one of these expressions and explain what it means.

_____

_____

How does the story help you know?

_____

_____

4. What were some participants in the study allowed to do that others were not allowed to do?

_____

Why do you think NASA scientists wanted some participants to do this?

_____

_____

Your Name: _____

Three Months at 6° *(cont.)*

Then   Reread the entire story one last time. As you read, think about how the story ends.

5. Sum up the last paragraph in just a few lines. _____

_____

_____

_____

6. How do you think Mr. Dang reacted when the students told him what they were doing?

_____

_____

Why might someone who had not been in the classroom earlier react differently than Mr. Dang?

_____

_____

7. Several of the people who were hired planned ahead. One man worked on writing a novel. Another man kept up a blog, had books to read, and knew what he was going to watch on television. What would you do for three months? Be specific. Keep in mind the information the story gives you about what you can and cannot do for the three months of the study.

_____

_____

_____

Would you hope to be one of the ones who exercised? Tell why or why not.

_____

_____

_____

**Learn
More**   Draw a stick-figure sketch of what you think a person running suspended horizontally on a vertical treadmill would look like. Look online to find a picture of the real thing and compare your drawing to it.

Key Search Terms

♦ vertical treadmill NASA

Scary Room in the Museum

 Something happens on the third floor of the Field Museum in Chicago, Illinois. It happens in an interior room without windows. To access this room, one has to go through two sets of thick doors. The room is inaccessible to the public. Many people find what goes on in this room to be terrifying and scary. Just the thought of it is enough to give them nightmares. There is no beating around the bush when it comes to what goes on in this room. The plain fact is that flesh is eaten.

 Anna Goldman is the woman who is responsible for managing this room, and she doesn't find it terrifying at all. When dead mammals are donated to the museum, it is Goldman's job to reduce each carcass to bones. It doesn't matter if the donated animal is a snow leopard, wild African dog, or a squirrel. Once the bones are cleaned, they can be studied by scientists or used for educational purposes. Goldman has assistants to skin the animals, but she still has to contend with the animal's brains and guts.

 For that task, Goldman relies on flesh-eating beetles. She says the beetles do a thorough job because "the beetles have tiny mouths that can chew into places in a body you would never imagine." The only parts the beetles won't consume are eyes or tongues. For that reason, eyes and tongues are hacked or cut out before being placed in the cage with the beetles. It ends up that these beetles detest those particular body parts because they are too moist.

 Although commonly known as flesh-eating beetles, the beetles are actually dermestid scavenger beetles. They are housed in nine cages, each one about the size of a home aquarium. The room is kept at about 75 degrees, and it is filled with spiders and spider webs. The spiders halt the beetle larvae from burrowing through the wooden frames around the cage lids. In addition, the webs make the beetles less eager to leave their cage.

 Goldman said mosquitoes were what first got her interested in insects. She was sent to a summer camp where she described finding herself to be "mosquito food." Instead of being upset, she wanted the mosquitoes to come to her so she could study and dissect them. Goldman started working at the Field Museum after she went to college.

Your Name: _____ Partner: _____

Scary Room in the Museum (cont.)

First — Silently read "Scary Room in the Museum." You might see words you do not know. It is likely there will be parts you do not understand. Keep reading! Determine what the story is mainly about.

Then — Sum up the story. Write the main idea and most important information. If someone reads your summary, that person should know it is this story you are writing about.

_____

_____

_____

_____

_____

_____

_____

After That — Read the story again. Use a pencil to circle or mark words you don't know. Note places that confuse you. Underline the main action or idea of each paragraph.

Next — Meet with your partner. Help each other find these words in the text.

access   inaccessible   carcass   hacked   detest

Read the sentences around the words. Think about how they fit in the whole story. Then match the words to their synonyms. Tell which part of the story helps you and your partner know you are right.

a. A synonym for *cut* is _____. I know because

_____

b. A synonym for *hate* is _____. I know because

_____

c. A synonym for *unreachable* is _____. I know because

_____

d. A synonym for *enter* is _____. I know because

_____

e. A synonym for *body* is _____. I know because

_____

Your Name: _____

Scary Room in the Museum *(cont.)*

Now   Answer the story questions below.

1. What happens to the bones once they are cleaned?

_____

_____

_____

_____

2. Why might a visitor to the museum not know about the flesh-eating room? Explain using facts from the story.

_____

_____

_____

_____

3. Near the end of paragraph 1, it says there is "no beating around the bush." What is meant by this expression?

_____

_____

How does the story help you know?

_____

_____

_____

_____

4. Is it likely that Goldman would ask someone to get rid of the spiders and their webs from the room? Why or why not?

_____

_____

_____

_____

_____

Your Name: _____

Scary Room in the Museum *(cont.)*

Then   Reread the entire story one last time. Think about how paragraph 1 and paragraph 5 relate to the story.

5. If you read only the title and the first paragraph, would you know for sure that this is a nonfiction story? Explain.

_____

_____

Why could it be the start of a fiction horror story?

_____

_____

6. Why might the author have begun the story this way? _____

_____

_____

Did you like the way it started? Tell why or why not. _____

_____

_____

7. If you had read the last paragraph first, would you have more likely known that this was a nonfiction story? Tell why or why not.

_____

_____

_____

How does knowing information about Goldman make the entire story less scary?

_____

_____

Learn More   Find in books or online five facts about beetles in general or specifically the dermestid scavenger beetle. On the back of this paper, write out your information in paragraph form.

Moment of Truth

 When Suzanna was asked why she didn't go to the water when she saw it, Suzanna's answer was well prepared. "Although I was parched with thirst, I still had control of my senses. I knew the closest oasis was over 100 miles away, and that meant that the water shimmering in front of me had to be a mirage. Light travels in a straight line, but it travels faster through warm air close to the ground than it does through cooler air above. When light slows down or speeds up, it bends in a new direction. You may see something straight in front of you, but bent light reaches your eyes from a different place than where it began. What I was actually seeing was the shining blue sky reflected onto the African desert!"

 When Suzanna was asked if she had encountered the haboob, she said that was what had gotten her into trouble in the first place. "As you know, the haboob is a strong wind that causes sandstorms in the southern areas of the Sahara. The one I faced lasted three hours. It was so strong that it made a wall of dense sand that was over 3,200 feet (1,000 m) high! It was terrifying to see it coming, and when it hit, it knocked me flat, buried my jeep, and I only survived by the skin of my teeth."

 When asked how she survived her encounter with the destructive wind and finally reached an oasis and water, Suzanna said, "Fortunately, I met some Bedouin nomads. They use camels to carry their tents and other possessions all around. I was tickled pink when they let me ride one. It was fantastic to be riding so high between the camel's two humps."

 "It's time for the Moment of Truth!" Mr. Chan said when Suzanna finished speaking. "You students all know the rules of the game. Was there anything wrong with Suzanna's story? She wins if you say there is nothing wrong but there is, and she also wins if you say something is false when it is in fact true. Yes, indeed, it's the moment of truth!"

 At first no one knew what to say, but then Jeremy's hand shot up. "Suzanna couldn't have gone to the Sahara Desert," he stated confidently. "She was correct about everything but the camels. Saharan camels are dromedaries, and they have one hump. Two-humped camels are Bactrian camels, and they live in central Asia."

Your Name: _____   Partner: _____

Moment of Truth (cont.)

First — Silently read "Moment of Truth." You might see words you do not know. It is likely there will be parts you do not understand. Keep reading! Determine what the story is mainly about.

Then — Sum up the story. Write the main idea and most important information. If someone reads your summary, that person should know it is this story you are writing about.

_____

_____

_____

_____

_____

_____

After That — Read the story again. Use a pencil to circle or mark words you don't know. Note places that confuse you. Underline the main action or idea of each paragraph.

Next — Meet with your partner. Help each other find these words in the text.

parched   shimmering   mirage   encountered   nomad

Read the sentences around the words. Think about how they fit in the whole story. Think about what the words must mean. Then mark each sentence as **T** (True) or **F** (False). Tell what information in the story helped you know.

_____ **a.** When something is **parched**, it is wet and moist. _____

_____

_____ **b.** When something is **shimmering**, it is dark and dull. _____

_____

_____ **c.** A **mirage** is a kind of optical (sight) illusion. _____

_____

_____ **d.** When you **encounter** someone or something, you avoid it. _____

_____

_____ **e.** A **nomad** stays in one place. _____

_____

Your Name: _____

Moment of Truth *(cont.)*

Now — Answer the story questions below.

1. Look at the pictures of the two camels. Which one is most likely to be found in the African country of Somalia? Fill in the circle beside the correct answer. Then use the lines to the right to explain your choice.

Ⓐ _____
_____
_____

Ⓑ _____
_____
_____

2. How does the game Moment of Truth work? Give at least three details about the game.

_____
_____

3. Suzanna says that she only survived "by the skin of her teeth." She also says she was "tickled pink" to ride a camel. Choose one of these idioms and explain what Suzanna means.

_____
_____

Which parts of the story helped you know? _____

_____

4. Tell what you would see in each instance:

a. If you saw a haboob approaching like the one in the story, what might you see?

_____
_____

b. If all of the air is the same temperature, would you likely see a mirage? Explain.

_____
_____

Your Name: _____

Moment of Truth *(cont.)*

Then) Reread the entire story one last time. As you read, think about how you read differently when you are looking for what is false and what is true.

5. In which paragraph do you find out that Suzanna is playing a game? Check the box.

❑ 1   ❑ 2   ❑ 3   ❑ 4   ❑ 5

How does the author give you this information? _____

_____

_____

_____

6. Is there any real proof in the story that Suzanna actually went to the Sahara Desert? Explain.

_____

_____

_____

Would you have liked the story better if you knew from the beginning that one of Suzanna's facts might be wrong? Tell why or why not. You cannot be wrong because it is your opinion, but you must explain.

_____

_____

_____

7. Imagine you are a contestant in the game Moment of Truth. Write a few lines about where you live or another place of your choosing. Do this in a way that is similar to how Suzanna talked about the Sahara.

_____

_____

_____

_____

Learn More) Find out more information about dromedary and Bactrian camels. On the back of the paper, create a chart comparing and contrasting the two. Think about where they live and how many there are, as well as how they are different physically.

Before George Washington

 One was found with an entire reindeer body in its stomach. Others have been found with the remains of polar bears, horses, and moose. Eight of them were 200 years or older. Scientists said one enormous female was at least 270 years old, but she actually could be 390 years old. That means that it is very likely that she was born before George Washington! Who are these creatures, and how were their ages determined?

 Although they have been called "the tortoise of the undersea world," they are actually Greenland sharks. Greenland sharks are scavengers. They are attracted to the smell of rotting flesh in the water. They can grow to over 20 feet long and weigh over 2,200 pounds. They have a very slow metabolism, and the reason they have been compared to tortoises is because they move so slowly. They usually cruise along at a speed of about half a mile per hour. Their top speed maxes out at about one and a half miles per hour. (To get a better feeling for how slowly they move, compare their speed to the average person's typical walking rate of three miles an hour).

 Scientists previously believed that bowhead whales were the longest living vertebrates. Now some say they were wrong. They say that the longevity prize for animals with backbones goes to the lethargic Greenland shark. To determine this, the scientists studied the eyes of these slow-moving sharks. They looked at the part of the lens that forms before birth. Then they measured the amount of radioactive carbon in that section of the lens. They used that measurement to extrapolate to the year the sharks were born.

 The scientists had to assume one thing before they could come up with the shark's age. They had to assume that a Greenland shark's size is related to its age. A scientist who was not part of the study did not agree. He said that assumption made the estimated ages "a bit of a stretch."

 The authors of the study defended their results. They said that their calculations showed that in most of the sharks they studied, age and size were closely related. The scientist who said the ages were a bit of a stretch did say that the study made a good case that the sharks can reach ages of 60 and up.

Your Name: _____   Partner: _____

Before George Washington (cont.)

First   Silently read "Before George Washington." You might see words you do not know. It is likely there will be parts you do not understand. Keep reading! Determine what the story is mainly about.

Then   Sum up the story. Write the main idea and most important information. If someone reads your summary, that person should know it is this story you are writing about.

_____

_____

_____

_____

_____

_____

After That   Read the story again. Use a pencil to circle or mark words you don't know. Note places that confuse you. Underline the main action or idea of each paragraph.

Next   Meet with your partner. Help each other find these words in the text.

previously   vertebrate   longevity   lethargic   extrapolate

Read the sentences around the words. Think about how they fit in the whole story. Think about what the words must mean. Then mark each sentence as **T** (True) or **F** (False). Tell which information in the story helped you know.

_____   **a.** When something is done **previously**, it is done before. _____

_____

_____   **b.** A **vertebrate** does not have a backbone. _____

_____

_____   **c.** Adult mayflies are known for their **longevity**, because they live for 24 hours.

_____

_____   **d.** When you feel **lethargic**, you have lots of energy and move quickly. _____

_____

_____   **e.** When a number is **extrapolated**, it is deduced or estimated. _____

_____

Your Name: _____

Before George Washington *(cont.)*

Now   Answer the story questions below.

1. What kinds of things have been found in the stomachs of Greenland sharks?

_____

_____

Are the items found in the stomachs of Greenland sharks proof that they are predators that kill their food? Defend your answer with evidence from the text.

_____

_____

_____

2. How did the scientists determine the sharks' ages?

_____

_____

3. One scientist says that it is "a bit of a stretch" when it comes to how the other scientists determined the ages of Greenland sharks. What does he mean when he says something is "a bit of a stretch"?

_____

Which parts of the story helped you know?

_____

_____

4. What do the scientists who did the study say about age and size when it comes to Greenland sharks?

_____

_____

_____

Would they likely say the same thing about people? Why or why not?

_____

_____

_____

Your Name: _____

Before George Washington *(cont.)*

Then   Reread the entire story one last time. As you read, think about how the title relates to the rest of the passage.

5.   How does the title help you understand how old the sharks are? _____

_____

_____

_____

Does the author assume or make an assumption that you know who George Washington is and his exact birthdate?

_____

_____

6.   If you only read the title, would you have any idea what the story is mainly about? Tell why.

_____

_____

Make a more general title and explain why it is a better title.

New Title: _____

Why It's Better: _____

_____

7.   Why is it good that scientists question each other's methods?

_____

_____

_____

How would you respond as a scientist if someone questioned your methods?

_____

_____

_____

Learn More   Find out more about the Greenland shark by looking in books or online. On the back of this paper, write down your information as five bullet points under the heading: Fascinating Greenland Shark Facts.

Reincarnation

 Molly, Paz, and Aaron were reviewing their new vocabulary word list for the week. "The first word on the list is reincarnation," Aaron said. "It means the rebirth of a soul in a new body or a new version or form of something from the past. The word has Latin roots. In Latin, *re* means 'again' and *carn* means 'flesh or meat'. . ."

 Paz interrupted, "I remember the root *carn*. It's in the word *carnivore*, and carnivores eat flesh! So reincarnation must mean that the flesh is made again. It's like a reinvention or a rebirth." "I don't believe in reincarnation," Paz said shaking her head, "but if I did, I would come back as a monkey or a giraffe."

 When Molly and Aaron asked why, Paz explained, "Monkeys are very agile, so if I came back as one, I could bend, twist, and move with ease. It would be easy for me to jump on all the furniture and swing from the curtain rods. If I was a giraffe, I could knock at your bedroom windows to get your attention. Then you could slide down my neck, and I'd take you for a ride!"

 The following weekend, Paz and her family went off for an overnight trip. Molly rode her bike to Aaron's house where they played a computer game. They didn't stop until they heard a loud din coming from the living room. When they rushed down to investigate the loud noise and clatter, their jaws dropped. It took them a moment to understand that the monkey swinging from the curtain rods and leaving a trail of destruction behind it was real and not something they were imagining.

 No one was sure where the monkey had come from, but the animal control officers said it had probably come from a traveling circus that had just arrived in town and was still setting up camp. Molly and Aaron texted Paz, who was amazed to hear their story. Later that evening, Molly and Aaron heard something knocking on Aaron's bedroom window. When Molly and Aaron turned to look, they were stunned at what they saw. It was a giraffe, and it was staring right at them.

Your Name: _____   Partner: _____

Reincarnation (cont.)

First   Silently read "Reincarnation." You might see words you do not know. It is likely there will be parts you do not understand. Keep reading! Determine what the story is mainly about.

Then   Sum up the story. Write the main idea and most important information. If someone reads your summary, that person should know it is this story you are writing about.

_____

_____

_____

_____

_____

_____

**After
That**   Read the story again. Use a pencil to circle or mark words you don't know. Note places that confuse you. Underline the main action or idea of each paragraph.

Next   Meet with your partner. Help each other find these words in the text.

reincarnation   carnivore   version   agile   din

Read the sentences around the words. Think about how they fit in the story. Define the words. Which information from the text helped you figure out the meaning of the words?

Word	Definition	Information That Helps
reincarnation		
carnivore		
version		
agile		
din		

Your Name: _____

Reincarnation *(cont.)*

Now   Answer the story questions below.

1. It never says directly, but can you infer which floor Molly and Aaron's bedrooms are on: the first or the second? Defend your answer with evidence from the story.

   _____

   _____

   _____

2. What information in the story helps you know that when you *reuse* something, you are using it again?

   _____

   _____

   _____

3. In paragraph 4, it says that Molly and Aaron's "jaws dropped." What is meant by this expression?

   _____

   _____

   Which part of the story helped you know?

   _____

   _____

   _____

4. A coincidence is a happening of events that seem to be connected but actually are independent of one another. A coincidence is an accidental occurrence. Could the events in this story be coincidences? Tell why or why not using evidence from the story.

   _____

   _____

   _____

   _____

   _____

   _____

Your Name: _____

Reincarnation (cont.)

Then Reread the entire story one last time. As you read, think about how the author uses foreshadowing. Foreshadowing is when a writer gives an advance hint of what is to come later in the story.

5. When you read the last line of the story, were you surprised? _____

_____

_____

_____

How was this line foreshadowed? _____

_____

_____

_____

6. Would the story have been as fun if it had been a squirrel at the window? Tell why or why not. Your answer cannot be wrong because it is your opinion, but you must explain.

_____

_____

_____

_____

7. What do you think was the author's main purpose for telling this story? Was it mostly to introduce vocabulary and Latin roots? Or was it to amuse the reader and get him or her to think about what was really happening? Give your answer and use evidence from the story to defend your claim.

_____

_____

_____

_____

_____

Learn More Find five words that begin with the Latin root *re*. Choose words that are not featured in the story. On the back of this paper, define the words.

Swimming Hot and Cold

 Her arms were completely numb, and she couldn't feel them at all. Hypothermia was a serious and dangerous risk. Normal body temperature is around 98.6°F (37°C). Hypothermia is a medical emergency. It occurs when your body temperature passes below 95°F (35°C). When your body is this cold, your heart, nervous system, and other organs can't work normally. If left untreated, one's heart and respiratory system may fail, and one will die.

 Lynne Cox was in 43°F water. Despite the intensity of the cold, Cox wore only a simple one-piece bathing suit and cap. She had nothing to protect her from heat loss. She had not smeared greasy lanolin on her skin, nor was she wearing a wetsuit. Cox had swum for 45 minutes in the chilling cold when suddenly the water changed to a hot 90°F.

 At first Cox was delighted in the warmer water, but then it turned back to the cold. Over and over this happened, and Cox said it was like "swimming across the strings of a guitar, each string or stream a different temperature." In the cold streams, when Cox needed to generate heat, she would swim faster and breathe every three to five strokes. The warm streams, although relaxing, added danger to Cox's swim. The contrasting hot and cold temperatures made it difficult for Cox's body to adjust to the cold. Because she couldn't acclimate, the cold water seemed even colder than it was. The warm water put Cox at a greater risk of hypothermia!

 How is it possible for water to change so suddenly? How could the temperature change be so extreme? Cox was swimming across Lake Myvatn. Lake Myvatn is in northern Iceland. No one had ever swum across the lake before because of the water temperature and the distance. The temperature changes came about because the lake has two different water sources. It is fed by icy streams of water that come down from the snow-covered mountains. It is also fed by geothermal rivers from deep below the lake. Geothermal energy is energy that comes from inside Earth.

 Cox's swim was successful. She swam across the lake in just under two hours. People in mittens, coats, and hats were waiting to cheer for her when she stepped out onto the black volcanic shore.

Your Name: _____

Swimming Hot and Cold *(cont.)*

For this activity, work in groups of four. If your group has fewer than four members, share the
Mr./Ms. Future task. Begin by deciding who will perform each task.

Title	Student's Name	What Is Your Task?
Mr./Ms. Meaning		Explain the meanings of unfamiliar words.
Mr./Ms. Plot		Summarize what is happening in the passage.
Mr./Ms. Ask		Ask important questions about the passage.
Mr./Ms. Future		Guess what will happen next in the passage.

First Read paragraphs 1–2 of "Swimming Hot and Cold." Then stop reading and do as follows:

Mr./Ms. Meaning: Explain the words *numb, hypothermia, organs,* and *smeared* to your group.

Mr./Ms. Plot: Summarize what happened in paragraphs 1 and 2. Tell how knowing what
numb, hypothermia, organs, and *smeared* mean helps you follow the plot.

Mr./Ms. Ask: Check to see if your group knows what is going on by asking a question about
water temperature and why Cox was at risk.

Mr./Ms. Future: Guess what is going to happen next. Why did the water temperature change?
Will it affect Cox's swim? Is she in danger?

Next Read paragraphs 1–4 of "Swimming Hot and Cold." Then stop reading and do as follows:

Mr./Ms. Meaning: Explain the words *delighted, acclimate, extreme* and *geothermal* to your group.

Mr./Ms. Plot: Remind the group about paragraphs 1–2. Then sum up paragraphs 3–4.

Mr./Ms. Ask: Ask a what/where/why/how question (one each) about Cox and her situation.

Mr./Ms. Future: Think about what Cox is trying to do. For how long will she swim? Will she be
successful? Will there be anyone to meet her when she comes ashore?

Then Read the entire passage from start to finish. As a group, do the following:

- Discuss the ending of the story. What would one's body feel like after swimming for two
hours in such cold water? How do you think the local people felt when someone came to
swim across the lake?

- Cox describes the water as "strings of a guitar." What does she mean by that?

- Does Iceland have mountains? Is the island volcanic? Quote words that help you answer.

- Talk about the author's purpose in writing this story. What do you think the author most
wanted you to learn from this story?

Finally On a separate piece of paper, write a short summary of your group's discussion.

Taxing Day

 "I want this to be a taxing day," Ms. Onerous said. When one of the students said nervously that they only had enough money for lunch, Ms. Onerous started to laugh. "I don't mean that you have to pay taxes today," she said. "I mean that I want the day to be taxing. I want it to be so demanding and challenging that you go home with a tired brain. I'm going to make you think really hard about language, the meaning of words, and word usage."

 The students looked at each other warily. They felt like they were treading in uncharted territory, and they weren't going to relax until they knew exactly what was expected of them. They began to get an idea when Ms. Onerous told them that although she would enunciate all the words very clearly, they might have trouble understanding what she said at first. This was because they would have to think about how words that are spelled the same might have different meanings.

 "The bandage was wound around the wound. The farm was used to produce more produce. The dump was so full that we had to refuse more refuse. Since there is no time like the present, he decided to present the present. I did not object to the object. I had to subject the subject to a series of tests." Ms. Onerous was silent for a moment, and then she said, "I'm going to repeat everything I said verbatim. Before I repeat it word for word, I want you to think about words that can be both nouns and verbs."

 After the class had discussed what Ms. Onerous said, Jack said, "I have two questions that don't deal with homographs or homonyms, but they will tax all of you. The first is, What do you get when you turn an elephant into a cat? The second is, Is it correct to say, 'The yolk of the egg *are* white?' or 'The yolk of the egg *is* white?'"

 William knew the answer to the first question. With a broad grin stretching across his face, he said, "a cat." As for the second question, Ms. Onerous started to explain subject-verb agreement, but she had to stop when the students started to laugh. Ms. Onerous didn't understand why they were laughing until they told her that the egg yolk is *yellow*.

Your Name: _____

Taxing Day *(cont.)*

For this activity, work in groups of four. If your group has fewer than four members, share the Mr./Ms. Future task. Begin by deciding who will perform each task.

Title	Student's Name	What Is Your Task?
Mr./Ms. Meaning		Explain the meanings of unfamiliar words.
Mr./Ms. Plot		Summarize what is happening in the passage.
Mr./Ms. Ask		Ask important questions about the passage.
Mr./Ms. Future		Guess what will happen next in the passage.

First — Read paragraphs 1–2 of "Taxing Day." Then stop reading and do the following:

Mr./Ms. Meaning: Tell your group what the words *taxing, warily, uncharted,* and *enunciate* mean.

Mr./Ms. Plot: Summarize what happened in paragraphs 1–2. Tell how knowing what *taxing, warily, uncharted,* and *enunciate* mean helps you know what is going on.

Mr./Ms. Ask: Check to see if your group knows what is going on by asking a question about what day it is and how the students are feeling.

Mr./Ms. Future: What will happen next? Will the day really be taxing? Are there words that are spelled the same but have different meanings? Can you think of any examples?

Next — Read paragraphs 1–4 of "Taxing Day." Then stop reading and do the following:

Mr./Ms. Meaning: Tell your group what the words *verbatim, homograph,* and *homonym* mean.

Mr./Ms. Plot: Remind the group what happened in paragraphs 1–2. Sum up paragraphs 3–4.

Mr./Ms. Ask: Ask for the meanings of the homographs and homonyms in the sentences Ms. Onerous repeated to the class.

Mr./Ms. Future: What are the answers to the two questions Jack asked?

Then — Read the entire passage from start to finish. As a group, do the following:

- Discuss the ending of the story. Did you like the answers to the riddles? Did you like that it was the students' turn to know and the teacher's turn to be confused?

- Discuss what the students meant when they said they were treading in uncharted territory. Have you ever felt nervous when you weren't sure about what you were going to do?

- Talk about how hard the English language is to learn. Talk about how even native speakers have trouble with homographs, homonyms, and things like subject-verb agreement. Talk about how difficult learning it must be for those who speak another language.

Finally — On a separate piece of paper, write a short summary of your group's discussion.

"Buried Alive" (pages 8–11)

Summary: A blizzard strikes, and a man has to bury himself in the snow to stay alive. After a long night, he is saved when he runs to what he hopes is the sound of a friend.

1. He was trying to simulate the conditions of a blinding blizzard.
2. It is probably not because we are told that the expedition was almost over (16 miles to go out of 3,725) and that blizzards strike often.
3. "fraught with danger" = "full of danger or unpleasantness"; "strike fast and furiously" = "happen very rapidly and with unrestrained energy"
4. He trusts that they will be out looking for him. Student illustrations should show five people tied together with a long rope.
5. Funatsu, as well as other scientists and explorers, practice over and over walking around with buckets on their heads to obscure their vision.

"Case Solved" (pages 12–15)

Summary: Ava and Ethan read a lot and use their knowledge to solve mysteries. Ava's knowledge of England and Ethan's understanding of cartography help them.

1. Rodney said the map was 150 years old. The X was below the *n* in *Iran*, but the country wasn't called Iran until 1935.
2. The steering wheels are on opposite sides. Student illustrations should show a driver on the right side of car in "England" box and one on left side of car in "United States" box.
3. She is being taken advantage of; her new "friend" is trying to cheat her by getting her to pay cash for a tour that does not exist.
4. The novel set in modern-day England; automobiles had not yet been invented in the 14th century, so there would be no mention of steering wheels.
5. Reading fiction and nonfiction can be interesting. Information one reads may help one solve cases or help people in real life; two cases are solved due to information in the current books being read.
7. Children in England are taught to look "right, left, right," because as Ava points out, the English drive on the opposite side of the road.

"Bark Ranger" (pages 16–19)

Summary: Bark Rangers are dogs trained to keep wildlife away from people in parks. They have helped to protect goats and to keep aggressive deer away from people.

Vocabulary: a. canines; b. frantically; c. distraught; d. congregating; e. bleated

1. mother = nanny or doe; baby = kid
2. They were licking up antifreeze from cars and eating trash people had left; the antifreeze was poisonous, and the trash could make them dependent on people.
3. To "lend a hand" is to help out, and dogs have paws instead of hands; the dogs are helping the park rangers keep wild animals away from people.
4. Yes, they cleared the parking lot better than when the rangers waved bags or shot empty shells into the air. They reduced the number of incidents from 40 to four when it came to aggressive deer. They helped rangers educate visitors, because the rangers could talk to the visitors when they came to pet the dogs.
5. paragraph 2
6. once or twice a week; they didn't want the goats to get used to Gracie like they got used to the people and cars.
7. The author gives background information, uses statistics (numbers), and provides quotes from experts.

"Updated Fairy Tale" (pages 20–23)

Summary: Students sum up a fairy tale in which a vain emperor is tricked into lying about seeing clothes that do not exist. The other characters go along so that he doesn't think badly of them. Only a little boy cries out that the emperor has no clothes.

Vocabulary: a. False; b. True; c. False; d. True; e. False

1. It can't be seen by those who are stupid, incompetent, or unfit for their positions.
2. There was no suit; no, because a good advisor would have bravely told the truth.
3. It means one is vain or self-centered; in the story, the emperor is vain, and all he cares about are his clothes.
4. She says their T-shirts are identical; they're the same size, color, and material.
5. One girl is teased because her T-shirt costs less than another girl's. Some students say they will cheer her up with the story "The Emperor's New Clothes."
6. It deals with modern issues such as teasing in schools and paying high prices for designer-label clothes.

"Eaten!" (pages 24–27)

Summary: Famous author and illustrator Maurice Sendak makes a drawing for a child fan, who then eats it. Sendak takes it as a compliment.

Vocabulary: hastily = "quickly"; lingered = "took his time"; recounted = "said what happened"; compassionate = "kind and caring"; rollicking = "very lively and amusing"

1. The sick lion mutters that he doesn't care, just like Pierre always does.
2. He did not, because otherwise he would not have spent so much time drawing it.
3. It is worth a lot; if a king were taken, one would have to pay a lot to get him back; it has to be worth a lot or else it wouldn't have mattered if he had eaten it.
4. It does not, because Sendak "could never end a tale on such a gruesome note." Illustrations might show the lion lying sick in bed and the lion visiting the doctor.
5. paragraph 2; yes, because most people have read or know about the book *Where the Wild Things Are*.
6. The drawing is eaten, Pierre is eaten, and though a minor detail, Max is sent to bed without eating; the title *Max* only focuses on a minor detail in the story.
7. Yes, because you would have known who the author was.

"Why Day" (pages 28–31)

Summary: A teacher confuses her students by giving them answers to questions. She matches one question to its answer, while the students match the others.

1. It will land on its feet; cat's lack a collarbone and have a very flexible spine, allowing them to twist, turn, and rotate so they can position themselves to land.
2. They run clockwise; Whitley had horses run the opposite of the way they did in Britain, and Whitley's horses ran counterclockwise.
3. They mean "get back to work" and "start thinking critically"; Ms. Trivia says the students must match answers to questions, as she did the first for them.
4. The smell comes from bacteria that feed on the sweat. Sweaty hands dry faster. Sweat doesn't evaporate on feet as quickly, especially feet in socks or shoes.
5. paragraph 2; she says, "I just answered four 'Why?' questions."
7. Even though it contains true facts, the story is fiction, because the teacher and her students are made up.

"Sampling Snot" (pages 32–35)

Summary: A scientist thought of using whale snot to find out about what is living in whale's lungs. Various methods are used to collect whale snot.

Vocabulary: massive = "huge"; obtain = "get"; specimen = "sample"; initial = "first"; bounty = "reward, a good thing to get"

1. They're using it to check what grows inside a whale's lungs (fungi, bacteria, viruses) and to analyze DNA, microbiomes, and hormones.
2. It can be used a half a mile away from the research boat, so there is no stress to the whale; it moves quickly and works automatically.
3. It means "not new, outdated"; after saying that is what the pole and the toy helicopter are, the story describes a much fancier and more advanced drone.

4. No, because it says that with shy, blue whales, Katrina had to use the helicopter. It says grey and sperm whales are more comfortable being close to boats.

6. Paragraphs 3 and 4 should be checked.

7. Paragraph 2 helps readers understand why getting the snot sample is so important; paragraph 5 gives readers a sense of how far science has progressed.

"Fair Swap?" (pages 36–39)

Summary: Janelle has traded her new shoes for a magic lamp and three wishes. She wishes for new shoes, a diamond, and an interview with Abe Lincoln. Her wishes come true, but not in the way she expects.

1. Students should draw a pair of new shoes, a diamond, and a picture of Lincoln.

2. It is set up like a baseball diamond; Young-Su asks her about it when he returns the shoes; she didn't know, because in the next line she says she doesn't like the way her wishes are turning out.

3. It means "to be nervously waiting to see what is going to happen"; Kyle speaks nervously, and he says he will feel this way until he finds out who is at the door.

4. She does not, because she could easily look up information about Lincoln. Despite that, she would give up one of only three wishes to talk to him.

5. *Janelle:* a girl who gets wishes; *Kyle, Duane, and Young-su:* friends of Janelle; *man at door:* man dressed like Lincoln; *setting:* Janelle's house, present time.

"King of Sting" (pages 40–43)

Summary: An entomologist developed a pain scale to rank insect stings. Two types of ant are discussed, along with information about the entomologist.

Vocabulary: embedded = "stuck in"; *entomologist* = "one who studies insects"; *forage* = "look for, gather"; *sluggard* = "slow-moving creature"; *potent* = "powerful"

1. He allowed himself to be stung 2,500 times by various stinging insects; pain is ranked from 1–4, with "4" being the most painful.

2. No, because Schmidt is an entomologist, and we are told he studies insects; no, we are told Schmidt focuses on ants, wasps, and bees.

3. Each person has his or her own opinion about something; some people may say that Schmidt is crazy, but he thinks he's just doing what he likes.

4. "One will start sweating, and the hair on one's arm will stand up like the hair on the back of a frightened dog's neck."

5. We don't yet understand everything about insect venom and its complex biochemistry. Perhaps it can affect our nervous systems in good ways.

6. The harvester ant's venom is 40 times more potent than that of a Western Diamondback Rattlesnake.

"Good Luck Bat" (pages 44–47)

Summary: A girl always strikes out, but then her uncle gives her a bat he says has powers. She becomes a great hitter, which she thinks is all because of the bat. Her uncle tells her the bat is ordinary. The next time up, she strikes out.

Vocabulary: dejected = "sad"; *listlessly* = "without energy"; *stowing* = "packing, putting away"; *purchased* = "bought"; *ultimate* = "last"

1. At the beginning, she strikes out all the time. Then she hits all the time with her uncle's bat. When she finds out the bat isn't special, she misses again.

2. Her uncle told her that a sorcerer said it had special powers, and she knew her uncle went deep into the Amazon jungle where there might be special trees.

3. a. Something amazes or surprises you. Samantha's uncle is amazed and surprised at how well she is hitting; b. We know the uncle does not literally mean that his socks have been blown off of his feet by how well she is hitting.

4. She struck out in the ultimate game even when she swung mightily and hard.

5. paragraph 4; he thought it was a matter of confidence, and now that she had proved that she was a good hitter, she didn't need it.

6. a. realistic fiction; b. magical realism

"Blubber How-To" (pages 48–51)

Summary: Blubber is a layer of fat that insulates animals from the cold and can also store energy. By conducting an experiment, one can see how blubber acts as insulation.

Vocabulary: insulation = "protective layer"; *frigid* = "icy cold"; *dual* = "two-fold, two"; *scarce* = "in short supply"; *conduct* = "perform, do"

1. It serves two purposes: as insulation against the cold and as stored energy.

2. The one in the plastic bags with the vegetable shortening; the vegetable shortening is an insulating layer of fat, like blubber.

3. It means that although an action may seem crazy, there is a reason behind it; it says it may seem crazy, but you find out why you turn the bag inside out later.

4. Students should shade in the box up to the 3/9 (or 1/3) mark; if the bag is too full, the shortening would spill out the top when you try to put the other bag and your hand in.

5. The title is unclear, there is too much information, and the steps are not numbered or clear enough; only paragraphs 3, 4, and 5

"Banner in the Sky" (pages 52–55)

Summary: A boy visits his grandfather and is angry at the lack of technology. He ends up liking one of his grandfather's books, which is about a boy who saves a climber.

Vocabulary: a. crevasse; b. tedious; c. flabbergasted; d. agony; e. aggravated

1. It will take too long, and the man will freeze to death before he gets back.

2. At first he thinks it is going to be of no interest because it is so old (1954, yellow pages), but then he gets really interested and doesn't want to stop reading it.

3. He is very angry; the boy is upset at being given a book to read instead of being able to do something on a computer, television, tablet, or smartphone.

4. It took a lot of strength to hold him and a lot of courage to try to save him.

5. It is called *Banner in the Sky* by James Ramsey Ullman, it was published in 1954, and the copy the boy is reading has yellowed pages and a torn cover; no, it could be anything: an original story, a news article, a dream, etc.

6. It was written in 1954, and he didn't think a book that old could be of any interest for him.

"Driverless Cars" (pages 56–59)

Summary: The author defends driverless cars. Most accidents are due to driver error, and we have the technology to change that. We shouldn't be afraid of change.

Vocabulary: prone = "likely to"; *hazardous* = "dangerous"; *innovation* = "modern improvement, change"; *novelty* = "new thing"; *eliminate* = "get rid of"

1. High wheelers: huge front wheel, small back one; safety: same-size wheels

2. Most accidents are due to driver error; she thinks they will reduce driver error.

3. If you really need something, you will invent it or find a way to get it; driverless cars are needed to reduce driver error, and we can do it with new technology.

4. People being afraid of change; we must embrace change, not fear it.

5. Paragraph 1 is mainly about people's fears in regard to the new safety bicycle; the author's purpose is to show that we should not be afraid of innovation.

6. Rhetorical question: "Why then did I mention people's objections to safer bicycles?"; answer: an opinion

"First Contact" (pages 60–63)

Summary: An anthropologist who studies isolated tribes gets lost on a reserve. The tribe forces him back to their camp.

Vocabulary: a. T; b. F; c. T; d. F; e. F

1. clothes, eyeglasses, and shoes

2. He was "drenched in sweat, scratched and bleeding, and covered in insect bites"; no, because everyone else could walk through the jungle with ease.

3. It means that something is in a risky or unstable situation; Dr. Bueno is not sure if the men are going to kill him or not, and he is helpless.

4. No, because she was in the reserve that was in a remote area. People there had never seen a road or even shoes, so there is no way a bike had ever been there.

5. A "modern" man is brought to Sheena's village. She asks her father what they will do with him, and he says they will take care of him because he is weak.

6. It is written as if it could be happening right now. There really are reserves for isolated tribes, and there are anthropologists who study them.

"Leg Burn" (pages 64–67)

Summary: A runner had to drop out of an ultramarathon because she was getting burns from her artificial leg heating up on the hot road. She returned another year to win. She began running at age eight, and losing the race or her leg has never stopped her.

Vocabulary: disqualified = "no longer allowed to compete"; *billed* = "called, named"; *prosthetic* = "artificial limb"; *grueling* = "really hard or difficult"; *allotted* = "given, allowed"

1. You are disqualified if you don't finish in 48 hours; yes, she was over two-thirds done when she dropped out, so she must have run for well over five hours.

2. Third-degree burns cause damage through every layer of the skin and require surgery, unlike a blister that can heal on its own.

3. It means "to have a bit less of something than is needed or expected"; she didn't quite make it to the 100-mile mark.

4. Yes, it says she started running when she was eight and lost her leg while driving a motorcycle. Most eight year olds aren't driving motorcycles!

5. paragraphs 1, 2, 3, and 4; paragraphs 5 and 6

6. Losing didn't matter because Amy found something that she loved to do.

"Three Months at 6°" (pages 68–71)

Summary: A teacher tells his class about a NASA job in which people had to lie flat in a sloping bed for three months. It is to study the effects of living without gravity.

Vocabulary: a. pensively; b. arduous; c. queries; d. literally

1. They are investigating the long-term effects on the human body of living without gravity; to do the job, people must stay in bed for three months at 6° downward slope, and also bathe, eat, and do bathroom stuff while in bed.

2. They burst out laughing; no, because they sat pensively and asked a lot of questions, and they found out that the job was really hard/uncomfortable.

3. "sound like a breeze" = it seems as if it will be really easy; "hammer" = asking questions fast and furiously, all at once

4. use a vertical treadmill; to see if exercise could counteract the effects of gravity

5. At lunch, the students make a plan. All together, they lay down on the floor with their supplies and tell their teacher they are practicing being astronauts.

6. He was likely pleased that the students had put thought and planning into their action; someone else might think they were being disruptive and disrespectful.

"Scary Room in the Museum" (pages 72–75)

Summary: There is room in a museum where flesh-eating beetles reduce animals to their bare bones. Spiders play a role in keeping the beetles in their cages.

Vocabulary: a. hacked; b. detest; c. inaccessible; d. access; e. carcass

1. They are studied by scientists or used for educational purposes.

2. on third floor, no windows, behind two sets of doors, not accessible to public

3. It means that one cannot discuss the matter without coming to the point; in the next line, you are told the plain fact that flesh is eaten.

4. No; the spiders keep the larva from eating the wood top frames, and the webs make the beetles less eager to leave the cage.

5. No; it has all the elements of scary stories where you don't really know what is going on, but it seems that there is something terrible that could harm you.

6. to hook you in, get you interested, and make you keep reading

7. Yes; it is biographical, and the tone is nonfiction.

"Moment of Truth" (pages 76–79)

Summary: Mr. Knowledge's class is playing a truth game. Suzanna's story is all true except for one detail about riding a two-humped camel.

Vocabulary: a. F; b. F; c. T; d. F; e. F

1. picture A; separate parts of the story tell us that the two-humped Bactrians are found in Asia and that the one-humped dromedary is found in Africa

2. People ask about where someone has gone and have to figure out if they're told the truth. They lose if they don't know what is true or false.

3. "by the skin of her teeth" = narrowly, just barely able to do something; "tickled pink" = really pleased or happy

4. a. a yellow, brown wall of sand as high as 3,200 feet high; b. no, because the light traveling through it would travel in a straight line and not bend.

5. pargraph 4; Mr. Dang says the students know the rules of the game.

6. No, but she obviously did her research.

"Before George Washington" (pages 80–83)

Summary: Greenland sharks are slow-moving scavengers. By studying their eye lenses, scientists determined that some live well over 200 years.

Vocabulary: a. T; b. F; c. F; d. F; e. T

1. parts of polar bears, moose, horses, and an entire reindeer; no, the story says that Greenland sharks are scavengers and are attracted to rotting flesh.

2. They measured the amount of radioactive carbon in the part of the eye lens that formed before the sharks were born.

3. He means it's a mild exaggeration beyond what is likely the case; he doesn't like one assumption, but he does say the sharks could live to be 60 or up.

4. They said that in most of the sharks they studied, age and size were closely related; no, because old people come in many heights, and they stop growing.

5. Washington was our first president and lived long ago, so you get a sense of something very old; expects you know Washington but not his exact birthdate.

6. No, it focuses only on a minor detail; a better title would reference sharks.

"Reincarnation" (pages 84–87)

Summary: Friends review the word *reincarnation.* One says she'd come back as two animals. While she's away, the others meet the animals. Both act as described.

Vocabulary: reincarnation = "a reinvention or a rebirth"; *carnivore* = "meat eater"; *agile* = "able to bend, twist, and turn"; *din* = "loud noise, clatter"

1. These must both be on the second floor, because a giraffe is tall, and Paz says, "You could slide down my neck" rather than "climb up on my back."

2. We are told that *re* is a Latin root that means "again."

3. They're shocked and amazed; what they were seeing was unbelievable.

4. Yes, because Paz is out of town and alive (she even texted them), and we are told that a traveling circus has recently come to town.

5. Paz says she would come back as two animals and describes what she would do. The monkey acts as she described, and so when there is a knock just as Paz said there would be, one is not totally surprised that it is a giraffe.

The lessons and activities included in *Close Reading with Text-Dependent Questions* meet the following Common Core State Standards for grade 6. (©Copyright 2010. National Governors Association Center for Best Practices and Council of Chief State School Officers. All rights reserved.)

The code for each standard covered in this resource is listed in the table below and on page 96. The codes are listed in boldface, and the unit numbers of the activities that meet that standard are listed in regular type. For more information about the Common Core State Standards and for a full listing of the descriptions associated with each code, go to *http://www.corestandards.org/* or visit *http://www.teachercreated.com/standards/*.

Here is an example of an English Language Arts (ELA) code and how to read it:

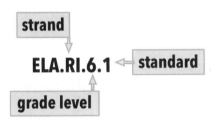

strand

ELA.RI.6.1 ← standard

grade level

ELA Strands

L = Language
W = Writing
RI = Reading: Informational Text
RL = Reading: Literature
SL = Speaking and Listening

+ +

Strand Language | **Substrand** Conventions of Standard English
ELA.L.6.1: Units 1–22
ELA.L.6.2: Units 1–22

Strand Language | **Substrand** Knowledge of Language
ELA.L.6.3: Units 1–22

Strand Language | **Substrand** Vocabulary Acquisition and Use
ELA.L.6.4: Units 1–22
ELA.L.6.5: Units 1–22
ELA.L.6.6: Units 1–22

+ +

Strand Writing | **Substrand** Text Types and Purposes
ELA.W.6.1: Units 1–20
ELA.W.6.2: Units 1–20
ELA.W.6.3: Units 1, 4, 15–16, 18

Strand Writing | **Substrand** Production and Distribution of Writing
ELA.W.6.4: Units 1–20

Strand Writing | **Substrand** Research to Build and Present Knowledge
ELA.W.6.7: Units 1–20
ELA.W.6.8: Units 1–20
ELA.W.6.9: Units 1–20

Strand Writing | **Substrand** Range of Writing
ELA.W.6.10: Units 1–20

+ +

Strand Reading: Informational Text	**Substrand** Key Ideas and Details

ELA.RI.6.1: Units 1–22
ELA.RI.6.2: Units 1–22
ELA.RI.6.3: Units 1–22

Strand Reading: Informational Text	**Substrand** Craft and Structure

ELA.RI.6.4: Units 1–22
ELA.RI.6.5: Units 1–22
ELA.RI.6.6: Units 1–22

Strand Reading: Informational Text	**Substrand** Integration of Knowledge and Ideas

ELA.RI.6.7: Units 1–2, 5, 8, 11, 13–14, 18
ELA.RI.6.8: Units 1–22

Strand Reading: Informational Text	**Substrand** Range of Reading and Level of Text Complexity

ELA.RI.6.10: Units 1–22

+ +

Strand Reading: Literature	**Substrand** Key Ideas and Details

ELA.RL.6.1: Units 2, 4, 6, 8, 10, 12, 14, 16, 18, 20, 22
ELA.RL.6.2: Units 2, 4, 6, 8, 10, 12, 14, 16, 18, 20, 22
ELA.RL.6.3: Units 2, 4, 6, 8, 10, 12, 14, 16, 18, 20, 22

Strand Reading: Literature	**Substrand** Craft and Structure

ELA.RL.6.4: Units 2, 4, 6, 8, 10, 12, 14, 16, 18, 20, 22
ELA.RL.6.5: Units 2, 4, 6, 8, 10, 12, 14, 16, 18, 20, 22
ELA.RL.6.6: Units 4, 8, 10, 12, 14, 16, 20

Strand Reading: Literature	**Substrand** Range of Reading and Level of Text Complexity

ELA.RL.6.10: Units 2, 4, 6, 8, 10, 12, 14, 16, 18, 20, 22

+ +

Strand Speaking and Listening	**Substrand** Comprehension and Collaboration

ELA.SL.6.1: Units 1–22
ELA.SL.6.3: Units 7, 9, 11, 15

Strand Speaking and Listening	**Substrand** Presentation of Knowledge and Ideas

ELA.SL.6.4: Units 7, 9, 11, 15
ELA.SL.6.6: Units 21–22